Walking Eye App

YOUR FREE EBOOK AVAILABLE THROUGH THE WALKING EYE APP

Your guide now includes a free eBook to your chosen destination, for the same great price as before. Simply download the Walking Eye App from the App Store or Google Play to access your free eBook.

HOW THE WALKING EYE APP WORKS

Through the Walking Eye App, you can purchase a range of eBooks and destination content. However, when you buy this book, you can download the corresponding eBook for free. Just see below in the grey panel where to find your free content and then scan the QR code at the bottom of this page.

Destinations: Download essential destination content featuring recommended sights and attractions, restaurants, hotels and an A–Z of practical information, all available for purchase.

Ships: Interested in ship reviews? Find independent reviews of river and ocean ships in this section, all available for purchase.

eBooks: You can download your free accompanying digital version of this guide here. You will also find a whole range of other eBooks, all available for purchase.

Free access to travel-related blog articles about different destinations, updated on a daily basis.

HOW THE EBOOKS WORK

The eBooks are provided in EPUB file format. Please note that you will need an eBook reader installed on your device to open the file. Many devices come with this as standard, but you may still need to install one manually from Google Play.

The eBook content is identical to the content in the printed guide.

HOW TO DOWNLOAD THE WALKING EYE APP

1. Download the Walking Eye App from the App Store or Google Play.
2. Open the app and select the scanning function from the main menu.
3. Scan the QR code on this page – you will then be asked a security question to verify ownership of the book.
4. Once this has been verified, you will see your eBook in the purchased ebook section, where you will be able to download it.

Other destination apps and eBooks are available for purchase separately or are free with the purchase of the Insight Guide book.

TOP 10 ATTRACTIONS

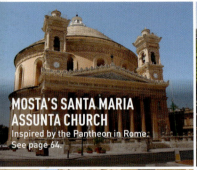

MOSTA'S SANTA MARIA ASSUNTA CHURCH
Inspired by the Pantheon in Rome. See page 64.

GOZO
This green little island has retained a more traditional lifestyle than its bigger neighbour. See page 70.

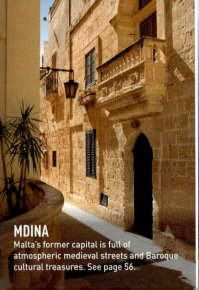

MDINA
Malta's former capital is full of atmospheric medieval streets and Baroque cultural treasures. See page 56.

THE BLUE GROTTO
Take in the dazzling azure waters of this lovely sea cave. See page 53.

ST JOHN'S CO-CATHEDRAL
The severe façade of this Valletta landmark belies the ornate beauty to be found within. See page 33.

MARSAXLOKK
The boats at this picturesque fishing port bear a painted eye to ward off evil. See page 51.

WATER SPORTS
The crystal-clear waters around the islands make Malta a popular choice for water sports enthusiasts. See page 89.

THE CITADEL, GOZO
An impressive structure. See page 74.

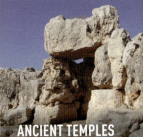

MELLIEĦA BAY
The best sandy beach on Malta, Għadira, lies on this beautiful bay, and borders a nature reserve. See page 69.

ANCIENT TEMPLES
Sites such as the 5400-year-old Mnajdra bear witness to Malta's unique early history. See page 53.

A PERFECT DAY

7.00am

Morning walk
Enjoy the early morning calm with a walk along Golden Bay. The beach is a tranquil oasis at this time of day.

11.00am

Exploring Mdina
Walk through Mdina and catch a showing of the Mdina Experience documentary, which offers an excellent overview of local history. Don't forget to take in the stunning view from the bastions before you go.

9.00am

Breakfast
Head to Crystal Palace (Triq San-Pawl) on the outskirts of Rabat for a tasty breakfast of *pastizzi*. This hole-in-the-wall establishment offers some of the island's best varieties of this traditional snack.

10.00am

Rabat 'train'
Hop on the Rabat 'train' which will take you around the outskirts of this rural area. Great fun and quite informative, too.

1.00pm

Palazzo Parisio
Head inland to Palazzo Parisio in Naxxar. This historic stately home is stunning and well worth a visit. After a tour of the palace, enjoy a delicious lunch in its lush Mediterranean garden.

N MALTA

pa time

s time to relax. St Julian's and Sliema have some
the island's best spas, such as the Fortina and the
ollo Day Spa. You can then sit back by the pool or
ead to sandy St George's Bay.

.00pm

alletta

alletta is bursting
ith culture, so use
ur afternoon to
ander through a
ouple of museums. St
ames Cavalier is ideal
r art lovers, while
e Grand Masters
alace makes you feel
s though you have
epped back in time.

7.30pm

Spinola Bay for dinner

Stay in the area for
dinner. Spinola Bay
is *the* spot for foodies,
with a great variety
of choices on offer.
Look for restaurants
that are packed with
locals.

9.00pm

Clubbing

Nearby Paceville is
the place to dance the
night away. The best
party clubs include
Footloose (St George's
Road) and the Havana
(also on St George's
Road), while Level 22
(Portomaso Business
Tower) and BarCelona
(Wilga Street) offer a
more sophisticated
atmosphere.

CONTENTS

INTRODUCTION

The tiny island of Malta sits at the heart of the Mediterranean Sea. Although only 316 sq km (122 sq miles) in area, its land has felt the ebb and flow of the most influential ancient cultures, and its people have witnessed pivotal moments in European history at first hand. Settled as early as 5200BC and coveted throughout its long history by the dominant power brokers of every age, Malta's amazing natural harbours have offered safety for some and contributed to disaster for others.

Six islands comprise the archipelago of Malta but only three are inhabited. Malta, the largest, is home to more than 400,000 people, while Gozo (known locally as Għawdex) has one-fifth of this population on an island a quarter of the size. Comino has a hotel and only a handful of houses, with no motorised vehicles, and the two St Paul's Bay islands see only day visitors. Finally, there is tiny Filfla, which witnesses only the footsteps of birds and lizards – as a nature reserve, no human visitors are allowed.

Harbour or honey?

The origin of Malta's name has long been debated. One theory is that it is a corruption of the Phoenician word *malat* (safe harbour), but for centuries the island was known as Melita, which is believed to derive from the Greek *meli* (meaning honey), a famous product of the islands in early times. Gozo (or Għawdex to local people, pronounced 'Ow-desh') is probably derived from the Greek *gaudos*, which in turn derives from the Phoenician word for a small boat.

LOCATION AND LANDSCAPE

Malta is the most southerly European country, situated

approximately halfway between the western and eastern ends of the Mediterranean, and roughly equidistant from the shores of Sicily and North Africa. It is believed to have been attached to Sicily until the end of the last Ice Age, when sea levels rose and washed in to part the islands.

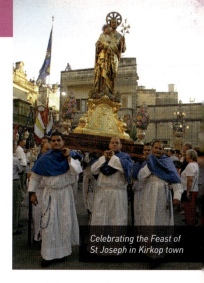

Celebrating the Feast of St Joseph in Kirkop town

Geologically, the islands are made up of layers of sandstone and limestone – a porous structure that has been eroded over the millennia by the power of wind and water. Hundreds of narrow coves have been cut into the coastline, interspersed with high cliffs and a few sandy bays. Ancient watercourses once flowed across the Maltese landscape, and these supported populations of dwarf hippopotamuses and elephants; hundreds of fossilised skeletons have been found in the cave of Għar Dalam in the south of Malta. Today the rivers have dried up, so Malta relies on winter rainfall, as well as a technologically advanced desalinisation process for its water supply.

In spring, the island's cliffs and rural waysides are awash with wild grasses and a plethora of attractive flowers. During the dry summer months, the hillsides grow parched and brown; the air is hot and still, and only the constant, loud chirping sound of the cicada (the Mediterranean's ubiquitous noisy insect) breaks the silence.

RICH HERITAGE

Settlers probably arrived here from Sicily as early as 5300 BC. They were a farming people, independent and self-sufficient. However, as soon as seafaring allowed greater mobility, Malta became an important port on the developing shipping routes, and this began a long tradition of control from abroad by the dominant Mediterranean maritime power in each successive era. In the 16th century Emperor Charles V gave Malta to the Order of St John, a military order of Knights Hospitallers. Malta was heavily fortified under the Knights' dominion. Their capital, Valletta, is now considered a masterpiece of late Medieval and Baroque architecture. In 1798 Napoléon Bonaparte evicted the Knights from their fortifications, but just two years later the French yielded to the British, who then ruled the islands – with some limited self-determination for its inhabitants – until 1964, when Malta gained independence. The islands were declared a Republic in 1974 and on May 1 2004, Malta officially became a member of the European Union.

⊘ FESTAS

Each settlement in the Maltese islands has its own saint's day or *festa*, generally over a weekend. The *festa* usually commences on a Saturday with a religious parade in which an effigy of the saint is carried through the streets, following a band. The community then takes part in a service at the parish church. The *festa* is not only a religious ritual, it also involves the participation of that most cherished of Maltese institutions, the local brass band, and there are huge firework displays, too. The streets are decorated and stalls sell drinks and food. Visitors are always welcome to take part.

PEOPLE

And what of the people who have lived so many centuries under the rule of foreign powers? They are some of the most welcoming people you could ever hope to meet. In AD 60 when St Paul arrived unexpectedly on the island as the result of a shipwreck off present-day St Paul's Bay, he received as warm a welcome from the people as visitors do today.

Blue Lagoon, Comino Island

Throughout the years, the Maltese have remained faithful to their own traditions and have retained a unique language and culture. Most of the local people speak Malti, the national language, which is closely related to Arabic. However, English is the second official language and is spoken by almost all. French and Italian are also widely spoken.

The Maltese and Gozitans (the people of Gozo) have a fierce loyalty to what they hold dear. Their Catholic faith is an anchor in their lives, and the pride of every village or town is its large, highly decorated parish church. Family relationships are close, and everyone displays respect for the older members of society.

Perhaps greatest of all is a love of their island, for which the Maltese fought so bravely during World War II that in 1942 Great Britain awarded them its highest award for civil bravery, the George Cross. They are proud of their independence, having one of the highest electoral turnouts in the world. More than 95 percent of the eligible population exercise the right to vote in elections, and they are vociferous in their opinions on the best way forward.

The Maltese don't spend all their time engaged in such serious and earnest pursuits though: they very much enjoy their relaxed island lifestyle. Whether it is a fisherman mending his nets or keeping his *luzzu* boat spic-and-span, or a waiter going about his business at the harbour-side restaurant, there is an unhurried air that helps the visitor to relax too.

Everyone knows everyone else and there is still a comforting network of mutual support here. If there is a new baby to show off, you will find both grandmothers proudly pushing the pram, basking in the warm congratulations of their neighbours. On Sunday whole families get together for a picnic or long lunch. Afterwards, the children play noisly while adults discuss current affairs.

CHANGES AND TOURISM

Although tradition still plays an important part in daily life, Malta has experienced a great deal of change since independence. Tourism has become the focus of wealth creation at a time of major population growth. As well as providing accommodation for local people and visitors, the resulting building boom has also put pressure on farmland and fishing communities. Much modern construction has been rather tasteless, and a preponderance of concrete blights most of Malta's resorts – although Gozo has wisely decided to carry on building in traditional sandstone. Meanwhile, the islands' membership of the EU has brought changes in the form of modern infrastructure.

The islands also have so much history – it's woven into the fabric of almost every Maltese building – that the accompanying responsibility can be quite problematic. But restoration plans for neglected historical sites and buildings are in hand and the islands' rich heritage is gradually returning to its former glory.

A BRIEF HISTORY

Situated at the heart of the Mediterranean Sea, Malta has long been an important island. It has played a key role in many of the world's major power struggles and has often been at the centre of key events in the history of Europe.

Civilisation dawned on the islands long before recorded history and the islands are rich in sites to explore. Settlers arrived on Malta during the Neolithic, around 5300BC, well after the end of the last Ice Age raised sea levels and separated the island from Sicily. They were farmers and brought wheat and a range of domestic animals with them. Archaeologists think that it was during this first wave of settlement that Malta lost all of its native forest.

It took almost another millennium for any great cultural development to take place, yet when it did, Malta saw the flowering of a sophisticated society, with a high level of building skills and complex rituals surrounding burial of the dead. From 4100BC, a thousand years before the earliest pyramids were built in Egypt, the first settlers began to construct towering free-standing stone structures, including Ġgantija on Gozo and

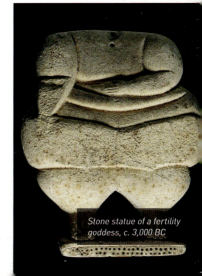

Stone statue of a fertility goddess, c. 3,000 BC

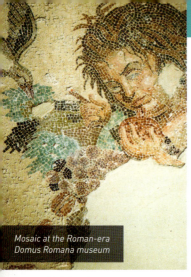
Mosaic at the Roman-era Domus Romana museum

Ħaġar Qim on Malta. The structures probably had wooden roofs and were likely used for religious ceremonies, granting them their current interpretation as temples. For example, the underground Hypogeum at Paola, where bones from more than 7,000 bodies were discovered in the burial chambers, has an oracle chamber that would likely have had a priestess present. The Temple Period lasted until 2500BC and its structures are now designated Unesco World Heritage Sites.

During the Bronze Age (2500–700BC), small settlements began to take shape. They remained undisturbed until the islands' harbours started to be used by the Phoenician traders in the late 8th century BC and island life began to change.

CARTHAGE AND ROME

The Phoenicians were great warriors as well as traders. From their base on the coast of Syria they travelled the Mediterranean and in time established a colony at Carthage in North Africa, dominating the whole region. Inscriptions, coins and tombs remain as a record of Phoenician control of Malta from 700 to 500BC.

When a new power, Rome, began to expand southwards, a clash with Carthage was inevitable. Three wars (the Punic Wars) were waged between 264 and 146BC until the Carthaginians were finally defeated. But by then Malta was already in the hands of Rome, having been taken in 218BC by a Roman expeditionary force. The Romans took over Mdina, fortifying it and building luxurious villas on the surrounding high ground. You can see the remains of a Roman house, the Domus Romana, in Rabat, outside Mdina.

ARABS AND CRUSADERS

As the Roman Empire went into decline, it was divided into western and eastern political administration. Malta was allocated to the east, governed from Constantinople, and became an important naval base. However, as Roman power declined, Arab influence grew, and after invading the islands in AD870, the Aghlabid emirs of Ifriqiyah (modern Tunisia) became the new rulers. One of their first actions was to build a fortified citadel at Mdina. Around AD909 the Aghlabids were overthrown by the Fatimid Caliphate, which was to extend its authority throughout much of North Africa in the first half of the 10th century.

⊘ ST PAUL'S SHIPWRECK

In AD60, one of Malta's most important historical events occurred. St Paul and St Luke were shipwrecked just off the island, somewhere in the area now known as St Paul's Bay. They had been travelling from Caesarea for trial in Rome, where Paul was to appeal to Caesar for clemency.

Paul spent the winter months in a cave at Rabat, where he preached Christianity, and his message began the conversion of the islanders. One of the first converts was Publius, the 'headman' of Malta, living in Mdina, who eventually became the island's first bishop.

Although the Arab rulers tolerated Christianity, many islanders emigrated, and some who remained converted to Islam. Two centuries of Arab rule left an indelible impression on Malta, especially

⊘ THE ORDER OF ST JOHN

The story of the Order of St John of Jerusalem (the Knights Hospitallers) begins in the 11th century, when Italian merchants obtained permission from the Muslim caliph to set up a Christian hospice in Jerusalem. Over time, the emphasis shifted to a military role, that of fighting for the faith. In 1187 the Knights were driven out of Jerusalem, and spent the following centuries fighting different Muslim leaders from their bases in Acre, Cyprus and Rhodes, before coming to Malta when they were given the islands by Emperor Charles V.

The Knights took vows of poverty, chastity and obedience. They were grouped in eight *langues*, or 'tongues', three of them French (France being divided in the 13th century into France, Provence and Auvergne). The other *langues* were Aragon, Castile, Italy, Germany and England. In Valletta, each *langue* built an *auberge*, where they lived together. Each *langue* was headed by a *pilier*, who had a set function: thus the *pilier* of Italy was Grand Admiral; the *pilier* of Provence was finance and ordnance manager; the *pilier* of France was head of the order's hospitals. Their head, the Grand Master, was elected for life and was subject only to the authority of the Pope.

As the years passed, corruption and internal dissent undermined the effectiveness and reputation of the Order. However, their place in history and their bravery in war have ensured their fame and honorary title: the Knights of Malta. Today, the organisation is known as the Sovereign Military Order of Malta.

on the language. Cotton and citrus fruits were introduced and became the mainstay of the economy as trade expanded.

In 1090, Count Roger I invaded the island from Sicily. The Norman conqueror had already taken Calabria with his brother and later succeeded in taking all of Sicily from the Fatimids in 1091. He struck a peace treaty with Malta, making the islands tributaries to his authority.

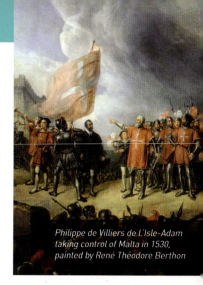

Philippe de Villiers de L'Isle-Adam taking control of Malta in 1530, painted by René Théodore Berthon

In 1127, his son, Roger II of Sicily, invaded again and took direct control, making Malta part of the Christian Kingdom of Sicily.

Malta was a key link in the line of communication during the Crusades, passing first through German and French hands before being taken by the Aragonese in 1282 and coming under Spanish rule. It was at this time that the Maltese nobility began to develop. In 1397 a system of local government called the Università was established and several local families became fundamental in its development.

THE KNIGHTS OF ST JOHN

The 16th century saw the Mediterranean Sea increasingly dominated by the Ottoman Turks, led by Sultan Suleiman the Magnificent. Their chief adversaries, the crusading Knights of the Order of St John, had long since been expelled from the Holy Land, yet still held onto a base on the island of Rhodes off the coast of Turkey. After repeated attacks and a six-month siege in 1522, the Turks took Rhodes on New Year's Day 1523. Rather surprisingly, Suleiman was merciful and granted the Knights leave to go. They were adrift again, but they departed with their wealth intact. Philippe Villiers de L'Isle Adam, the courageous Grand Master of the Order, led his soldiers from their home to Sicily and to Italy, where for eight years they were without a base. Eventually, the Holy Roman Emperor, Charles V, offered the island of Malta to them, and in 1530 the Grand Master and his 4,000 men moved to this new base. At that time the islands had around 12,000 inhabitants.

The Knights built fortifications and living quarters in the great harbour at Birgu (later called Vittoriosa) and the neighbouring peninsula, Senglea. As the Grand Harbour area became the focus of activity, so the importance of the old capital, Mdina, declined. When the Spanish Inquisition arrived on the island in 1561, the Inquisitor's Palace was built in Birgu.

The Knights had not seen the last of the Turks, however. Suleiman regretted his charitable act and, soon after the Knights arrived in Malta, was plotting to take over the island and its strategic position. Suleiman considered the Order of St John his old enemy and the islands his stepping-stone to the invasion of mainland Europe. The Knights also found themselves threatened by privateers from North Africa, under the command of one Dragut. They devastated Gozo in 1546 and took thousands of Gozitans as slaves in 1551. And then Dragut joined forces with the rampaging Turks.

THE GREAT SIEGE

In 1565, when word reached Grand Master La Valette of a huge force approaching his islands, he sent out desperate appeals for help. Only a small number of volunteers came. On 19 May,

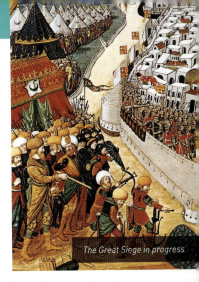

The Great Siege in progress

a Turkish fleet of 181 galleys disembarked an army of 30,000 at Marsaxlokk Bay. Among them were 4,000 fanatical janissaries, mostly converts to Islam, the crack troops of their time. The invaders, with the navy commanded by Admiral Piali and the army by Mustapha Pasha, were confident of victory. La Valette had only his 600 knights, 1,200 infantrymen and a militia of about 5,000 untrained men and slaves, as well as eight galleys. These men were to prove astoundingly resilient, as they performed one of the most valiant defences in history.

Throughout the summer of 1565, heat, disease and diminishing food supplies plagued both sides as they battled on. The Maltese people fought and suffered along with the Knights in fierce resistance. Each man lost was irreplaceable, and strategic positions were abandoned one by one for lack of troops to hold them. At one critical point, La Valette himself, although he was aged 72, threw himself into the fray, inspiring his followers by his courage. The valiant defenders gradually wore down the Turks, despite their advantage. Arguments between the two Turk commanders did not help. In one assault alone on Senglea, the Turks lost 2,500 men.

At last, a relief force from the Viceroy of Sicily came to the rescue. On 7 September, under Don Garcia de Toledo, they landed at Mellieħa Bay. The Turks were fooled into believing the fresh troops to be more numerous than they really were, and they therefore abandoned the siege. As the remnants of the Turkish forces sailed away, their defeat marked the turning point in Ottoman fortunes, and their empire began a slow decline. In Malta there was great rejoicing, although the island was devastated by the siege.

Money poured in from grateful Christian monarchs around Europe, relieved to have been saved from the threat of further Muslim expansion. Plans were drawn up for a new city across the harbour facing Birgu, on the Sceberras peninsula that separates the island's two great harbours. This position could be more easily defended in any future conflict. The Order obtained the services of the Pope's own architect, Francesco Laparelli. The capital was to be called Valletta – after the resolute Grand Master La Valette (the double L comes from the Italian version of his name). Its modern, grid design allowed for easy movement and cooling breezes, something lacking in the design of medieval Birgu. The plan of the city inspired Maltese architect Gerolamo Cassar. He is responsible for much of the way Valletta looks today, with fine, harmonious buildings blending early Baroque with classical elements.

By the 18th century, much of the Mediterranean was in the doldrums. New trade routes to the riches of the East, around the Cape of Good Hope, and from the Americas and the Caribbean brought new cargoes, and consequently took all the best investment. Without their old enemies, the Ottoman Turks, to fight against, the Order seemed to lose its focus, becoming dissolute and tired. The French Revolution of 1789, and the subsequent downfall of the aristocracy and the church in France, shook the Order to the core, for it deprived the Knights of much of their support – and a major part of their revenue.

The grid design of Valletta

ENTER NAPOLEON

In 1798, Napoleon Bonaparte avariciously eyed the Mediterranean and came to the same conclusion reached by many commanders before and since: Malta would be valuable to him, and
it would pose a serious threat if it were to fall into the hands
of his enemies. On 9 June his armada of 472 ships carrying
5,000 soldiers gathered along the coastline and, on the pretext
of entering the harbour for provisions, Napoleon landed with
some troops. He presented the Knights with a simple order: they
must pack up and leave. Where others had failed, Napoleon succeeded. Grand Master von Hompesch had no stomach for a fight
and simply did as he was ordered. After 268 years in residence,
the world's most famous military order departed without any
action to defend its stronghold.

Two years of French rule followed, in which the arrogant
behaviour of the occupiers made them hated by both the Maltese

and the Church. A popular insurrection began, and as the Maltese began to rebel, so a delegation was sent to Naples to request help from the British Navy, which was based there while preparing to pursue and destroy the French fleet. Britain was at war with France and, appreciating the islanders' need for help in their uprising, both the king of Naples and Admiral Horatio Nelson sent troops and ships to Malta. The islands' harbours were blockaded by the massed ships, and troops were landed. Against such odds the French commander surrendered and the French force left the islands, taking with them many treasures they had looted. On 5 September 1800 the British flag flew over Valletta.

Britain informally administered the islands for the remainder of the ongoing Napoleonic Wars and British possession of the islands was formally recognised in the Treaty of Paris in 1814, and again at the Congress of Vienna.

British ship in Grand Harbour

BRITISH COLONY

In 1813 – a year marked by a plague that killed off one-fifth of Malta's inhabitants – Sir Thomas Maitland arrived as governor. Nicknamed 'King Tom', he dismissed the traditional self-governing Università and introduced sweeping reforms to bring the legal system into line with the English one. A period of stability followed, which saw new crops introduced, more vineyards planted, and water resources managed more efficiently, resulting in increased crop yields. The building of bases for the Royal Navy that patrolled the expanding British Empire boosted both employment and prosperity. The opening of the Suez Canal in 1869 increased shipping in the Mediterranean, and by 1880 Grand Harbour was a major port.

The George Cross

In recognition of the bravery and sacrifice shown by the Maltese in World War II, the island was awarded Britain's highest honour for civilian gallantry – the George Cross. It is shown on the national flag.

The Maltese, however, had not lost their desire to achieve independence, and during the 19th century a succession of constitutions gave the people varying degrees of autonomy. Riots following World War I brought about real change, codified in the new constitution of 1921. The Maltese became responsible for their own internal affairs, while London retained control of defence, foreign affairs and matters affecting the Empire.

WORLD WAR II – THE SECOND GREAT SIEGE

Malta was vital to the Allied cause during World War II. Not only could ships and aircraft based here block the deployment of Italy's navy, they could also attack supply routes to the German and Italian forces operating from North Africa. When Italy under Benito Mussolini entered the war on 10 June 1940, his first move was to bomb Malta. During 1941, Italian, and later German, aircraft kept up almost incessant daily raids.

As General Rommel advanced through Egypt in the spring of 1942, air attacks increased, and in March and April the islands were hit with more than twice the weight of bombs that fell on London during any full year of the war. Life became increasingly miserable, with people living in cellars and caves in conditions of near-starvation.

This second great siege in Malta's history was only relieved in August 1942 with the arrival of a convoy of ships carrying fuel and supplies. Just five of the 13 ships sent from Britain made it, but it was enough to save the island and the Allied foothold in the area.

INDEPENDENCE

The price of freedom had been high: thousands of people killed or injured, and thousands of homes destroyed. After the war, Britain gave Malta financial help for reconstruction, and a new constitution granted the islands self-government within the Commonwealth. Plans for the complete transfer of power met with difficulties, but on 21 September 1964, Malta became fully independent. Her parliament declared a republic in 1974. In 1979, British forces bade farewell to Malta. Although the islanders welcomed independence, many had depended on the forces for their livelihood, and the island needed to find other forms of revenue.

Tourism seemed a perfect choice. The kind climate, along with the wealth of historical buildings, would guarantee visitors, and Malta benefited from the growth of air travel in the 1970s and 1980s. The rush to develop a tourist infrastructure has not always resulted in the best-planned or prettiest resorts, but in the 1990s Malta began to make efforts to do justice to its architectural beauty. Malta joined the European Union in May 2004, taking its place alongside much larger member countries with a mixture of enthusiasm and trepidation, and on 1 January 2008 the euro was introduced. Change was in the air and funds were ploughed into Valletta's regeneration, which was eventually completed in 2015. Several ambitious new projects are in the pipeline too, which will prepare the capital for 2018 when it becomes the European Capital of Culture.

HISTORICAL LANDMARKS

5300 BC Settlers arrive, probably across a land bridge from Sicily.

4100 BC onwards The first temples are built.

550–218 BC Malta is ruled by Carthage, a former Phoenician colony.

218 BC The islands become part of the Roman Empire.

AD 60 St Paul and St Luke are shipwrecked off Malta.

5th and 6th centuries Malta is conquered by Goths and Vandals.

870 The islands are conquered by the Aghlabid Caliphs.

1282–1530 Aragonese rule Sicily and Malta.

1530 Emperor Charles V gives Malta to the Order of St John.

1546 and **1551** Privateers from the Barbary Coast attack Gozo.

1565 The Great Siege. Suleiman the Magnificent's Ottoman fleet lays siege to Malta for three months, but is unsuccessful.

1566 Construction work begins on the new capital, Valletta.

1798 Napoleon takes Malta without a fight. The Knights are forced out.

1800 The Maltese call the British fleet under Admiral Nelson to their aid. The islands' British period begins.

1869 Suez Canal opens with Malta at the forefront of Mediterranean trade.

1921 Britain grants Malta its own constitution and partial self-government.

1934 Maltese becomes an official language alongside English.

1939–43 Malta is severely bombed in World War II. In acknowledgement of the islanders' heroism, Britain awards the islands the George Cross.

1964 Malta gains its independence in the Commonwealth.

1974 Proclamation of the Republic of Malta.

2004 Malta becomes a member of the European Union.

2008 Malta adopts the euro. Ruling Nationalist Party wins elections.

2010 Works start on Valletta's iconic City Gate project.

2012 Pjazza Teatru Rjal (the site of the old opera house) opens for the first time since World War II.

2013 Labour Party wins the snap election and returns to power after 15 years.

2014 Hundreds of migrants drown as their boats capsize off Malta's coast.

2015 The regeneration of Valletta's city centre is finally completed.

2018 Valletta will be the European Capital of Culture.

The new City Gate and Parliament building, designed by Renzo Piano

# WHERE TO GO

The Maltese Islands are compact and relatively easy to explore either independently in a rental car, on public transport or by an organised tour. We begin by looking at the largest island, Malta – including Valletta, the towns around it, and the Grand Harbour. Other sections of the book will explore the southeast coast before moving inland. Finally, we will journey along the northern coast before sailing across the water to Gozo, and paying a brief visit to Comino.

VALLETTA

When the Order of St John first settled on Malta in 1530 they made their home at Birgu (today's Vittoriosa) in the Grand Harbour where the Maltese community lived. It was sheltered and had deepwater creeks for merchant ships. Across the harbour, separating it from the equally large Marsamxett Harbour with its fishing community, lay the barren Sceberras peninsula with a small fortress, Fort St Elmo, at its tip. As the fort guarded the entrance to the harbours, they set about reinforcing its battlements to make it impregnable.

In 1565, however, when the Ottoman force landed, it set up its mortars on the peninsula's high ground and rained fire onto St Elmo below. The Knights and

Balcony views

In the 18th century, to give privacy to wives and daughters watching daily life in the streets, many city buildings were furnished with *gallarija*, wooden balconies. Lines of these colourful balconies form one of the city's most enduring images.

their Maltese compatriots put up some courageous resistance, but ultimately all but four of the defenders were killed. The Turks then turned all their fire on to the fortified community that lay across the harbour – Birgu, Bormla (today's Cospicua) and l'Isla (Senglea). The Knights were finally victorious and the siege was lifted, but lessons had been learned. Plans were speedily made to create a new fortified city on the dominating heights of the peninsula. The city would be called **Valletta ❶** in honour of Grand Master La Valette who led the islands to victory.

A simple yet effective design was created. The city would have towering bastion walls encircling it, with two defensive emplacements known as Cavaliers where troops would be stationed, overlooking a dry moat near the land-side entrance to the city. The newly restored, much larger Fort St Elmo would guard the sea approach. Within the city walls all streets would run in a grid pattern with palaces, churches and the *auberges* where each group of knights or *langue* would live, given due prominence. It would be a gracious city, built with the generous monies sent by the grateful monarchs of Europe who had seen the spread of the Ottoman Empire so successfully halted.

Ancient Malta

A timeline close to the doorway of the National Museum of Archaeology points out that the Maltese temple sites were built over 1,000 years before the pyramids in Egypt.

Work began in 1566 from plans drawn up by Francesco Laparelli, architect to the Vatican and the Medici family. He promised that the city could be constructed in a mere three months, but when he returned to Italy two years later there was still a great deal to be done. The project was left in the hands

Fort St Angelo

of his Maltese assistant, Gerolamo Cassar, who finished the work, and also added his own imprint on the city.

Following the departure of the Knights of St John at the end of the 18th century, many of Valletta's beautiful buildings were taken for other civil or military uses. Today, the initial *raison d'être* for the creation of the city can still clearly be seen. The walls and bastions still stand firm, and to see the city from the air, or from the waters of the Grand Harbour or Marsamxett Harbour, really brings home the amazing feat of the builders. In 1980, the city of Valletta was designated a Unesco World Heritage Site.

CITY GATE

Valletta is less than 1km (0.6 miles) wide and 1.5km (1 mile) long. The main entrance, known as **City Gate**, has been replaced twice since the original Baroque gate was erected, firstly in the 1960s with an archway of little architectural value, and more recently by renowned Italian architect Renzo Piano, as part of the island's Vision 2015 initiative. The project involved the remodelling of the entrance to the old city, the new parliament building, a piazza and a new performing space. The new City Gate is a modern structure, which bares similarities to the ancient Egyptian temple of Edfu. The new **Parliament House**, inaugurated in 2015, is an environmentally friendly building consisting of large, porous blocks connected by bridges. The building has attracted sharp criticism for being expensive, ugly and allegedly unnecessary. Nevertheless, it has quickly become symbolic of the city's transformation. More infrastructure projects, such as the regeneration of the covered market is-Suq l-Antik tal-Belt, the new Valletta Design Cluster in the old civil abattoir and the New Museum of Art (MUZA) at the Auberge d'Italie, are due to be completed by 2018, when Valletta becomes the **European Capital of Culture**.

The gate sits at the top of the main road through the city, **Triq ir-Repubblika** Ⓐ (Republic Street), and exploring its attractions makes a good start for a tour. The upper section is relatively flat, then drops down towards Fort St Elmo jutting out to sea. It is a pleasant thoroughfare with several fine buildings as well as shops and cafés along the way.

Strolling down the street, which was known as Strada Reale during the Knights' days and Kingsway under British rule, you will first notice the ruins of what would have been a large building; vestiges of classical columns can still be seen. This was the site of the **Royal Opera House**, which was bombed in 1942 and never rebuilt. Now, as part of the City Gate project, the site has been revamped into a modern open-air theatre, known as **Pjazza Teatru Rjal** (Royal Theatre Square), which will be the new venue of the annual Valletta International Film Festival.

Further along you will find the Auberge de Provence, finished in 1575 and housing the **National Museum of Archaeology** Ⓑ

Inside St John's Co-Cathedral

(www.heritagemalta.org; daily 9am–5pm, until 6pm Mar–Dec). The building itself is interesting, being one of the *auberges* that the public can still enter. The collections it displays are fascinating and add extra detail to the bare bones of the islands' pre-historic times, with the Neolithic and Bronze ages being brought vividly to life. Beautiful pottery effigies and stone carvings found at Tarxien (see page 49) and other archaeological sites bear witness to the sophistication of these ancient peoples. Upstairs, the collection focuses on later periods, featuring finds from the Roman era.

ST JOHN'S CO-CATHEDRAL

Next you come to one of the most important buildings in Valletta, the **Co-Cathedral of St John** Ⓒ (www.stjohnscocathedral.com; Mon–Fri 9.30am–4.30pm, Sat 9.30am–12.30pm) dedicated by the Knights to their Maltese architect Gerolamo Cassar (entrance on Republic Street, opposite the Law Courts). Cassar's design for the church, which was constructed between 1573 and 1577, surrounded the building with a number of small open squares. The severe facade of the cathedral belies the ornate beauty within – it is a magnificent decorative masterpiece. Small chapels off the main nave are dedicated to each *langue*, and the floor of the church consists of Knights' tombs, highly embellished with coloured marble. The vault is decorated with several huge frescoes by Mattia Preti (1613–90), an Italian artist favoured by the Order, featuring scenes from the life of St John the Baptist.

The church, which was granted cathedral status by Pope Pius VII in 1816 (the name Co-Cathedral indicates it belonged to a convent or religious order), also has a museum with beautiful Flemish tapestries and other works of art, including Malta's greatest treasure, *The Beheading of St John the Baptist*, by Caravaggio. It is a masterpiece of great dramatic intensity and the only work by Caravaggio to bear his signature.

REPUBLIC SQUARE

Beyond the cathedral on Republic Street you find **Republic Square**, centred on a solemn statue of Queen Victoria, usually sporting a pigeon atop her tiny crown. In fine weather she is surrounded by a sea of parasols and café tables, where you can enjoy lunch or a drink and watch the world go by. The buildings on the square are beautifully colonnaded but the eye is drawn to an ornate facade in its backdrop. This fine

Living history

Valletta Living History (Embassy Shopping Complex, St Lucia Street; daily 10am–3.15pm) is a 35-minute docu-drama that takes its audiences on a whirlwind tour of the city's past, and includes titbits of fascinating information.

Baroque building, the last to be constructed by the Knights, was finished in 1796. Originally intended to house the collection of books owned by the Order, it is now the **National Library** (1 Oct–15 June Mon–Fri 8.15am–5pm, Sat until 1.30pm, 16 June–30 Sept Mon–Sat until 1.15pm; free). For those with a particular interest in the Knights of St John, the library is a treasure trove

Queen Victoria statue in Republic Square

of information and artefacts. In addition to a large collection of books, including more than 45 printed before 1500, there are charters and documents relating to the workings of the Order, including the original Deed of Donation of Malta to the Order in 1530. Many of the oldest books, some dating back to the 12th century, can now be downloaded from the digital archive (http://digivault.maltalibraries.gov.mt).

PALACE OF THE GRAND MASTERS

Next to Republic Square is the huge facade of the **Palace of the Grand Masters D**, once the official and private residence of the Grand Master of the Order of St John. The renovated Palace Square opposite is the perfect place to sit and admire its beautiful exterior. The palace, with a 100-metre (109yd) -long facade, was constructed between 1572 and 1580 with one entrance arch (near Archbishop Street). Later in the 18th

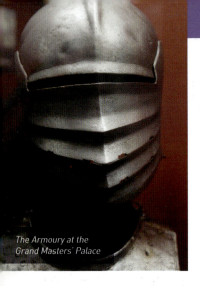

The Armoury at the Grand Masters' Palace

century Grand Master Pinto added the second entrance and the long balconies that grace each corner. Today the palace is the president's office and seat of the Maltese Parliament.

A visit to the **State Rooms** (tel: 2124 9349; daily 10am–4pm), like a visit to St John's Co-Cathedral, brings to life the wealth and power of the Order of St John. Overlooking Neptune's Courtyard, the fine rooms of the *piano nobile* (first floor) are linked by corridors decorated with frescoes, armour and portraits. An impressive door leads into the **Throne Room**, also called the Hall of St Michael and St George, the Order's Supreme Council Chamber. Its frieze depicts 12 incidents in the Great Siege. To one side is the **Red Room**, which was the Grand Master's audience chamber, and to the other, the **Yellow Room** where pages would wait to be summoned. Also here are the **State Dining Room** and the **Tapestry Chamber**. The Gobelin tapestries on the walls were presented in 1697.

On the ground floor is the **Armoury** (www.heritagemalta. org; daily 9am–5pm). The collection of 6,000 pieces includes remarkable suits of armour made for Grand Masters, arms used in the Great Siege of 1565, and a rare hide and copper cannon, along with pikes and shields. Grand Master Wignacourt's ceremonial suit is inlaid with gold.

North of the palace, Republic Street drops down towards Fort St Elmo. A series of wide marble steps flank the roadway; be careful, they can be slippery in wet weather. At No. 74 Republic Street you'll find **Casa Rocca Piccola** (www.casaroccapiccola.com; daily 10am–4pm), built in the 16th century and now the home of a noble family. The interior is typical of secular architectural design at the time, including an interior courtyard with stairs leading to a *piano nobile* or first-floor living area. The rooms are full of antiques, including a portable altar that folds neatly into a chest of drawers for travelling. As of 2017, guests will have the option to stay overnight in the one of the carefully restored guest rooms.

FORT ST ELMO

Where the road ends you reach **Fort St Elmo Ⓔ**. This huge fortification – pride of the Knights of St John – was rebuilt and extended after being overrun in the siege of 1565 and was further fortified in 1687. The round stone slabs at the entrance to the fort are the covers of huge underground grain stores, each of which could hold 5,000 tons of food. Flat stones shield the openings against rain and prevent visitors from falling into the stores. The fort, which was upgraded several times during British rule, last saw action in World War II and shows evidence of almost every era of its existence.

Vendome Bastion, a part of the fort once used to store gunpowder, is now the **National War Museum Ⓕ** (www.heritage malta.org; daily 9am–5pm, until 6pm in summer). Enter through an arch some 50 metres (54yds) west of the fort's main entrance. The museum, dedicated in 1975, tells the story of Malta's second great siege in World War II, and her role in the Allies' eventual success in 1945. Photographs show the devastation caused by Axis bombing, and relate stories of heroism by Maltese nationals and servicemen. Hundreds of relics are on view, from the Gloster Gladiator biplane 'Faith' – one of only three on hand to protect the island at the start of hostilities – to ration books and gas masks. Pride of place goes to the **George Cross**, awarded to Malta in 1942 in recognition of the islanders' bravery in the face of continued attacks.

MARSAMXETT SIDE OF REPUBLIC STREET

After exploring the attractions along Republic Street, head out to the other parts of the city. The places of interest are not difficult to find on the narrow streets, so turn first to those on the streets to the left of Republic Street (the northern Marsamxett side), then to the right (southern, Grand Harbour side).

As the threat of the Turks subsided, the Knights began to look for worldly pleasures to fill their time and in 1731, the Grand Master, Manoel de Vilhena, commissioned a theatre for the city. The **Manoel Theatre** (Teatru Manoel; www.teatrumanoel.com.mt) opened a year later and presented plays and operas until the Royal **Opera House** opened in 1861. The latter was bombed during World War II then converted in 2013 into an open-air theatre (see page 32), while the Manoel, in Old Theatre Street, having fallen into disrepair, was completely refurbished at government expense in 1960. Today its beautifully decorated stalls and elliptical ceiling are well worth seeing, as are its theatrical productions. There are regular guided tours so you don't need to wait for a performance. Alongside the theatre and dominating the Valletta skyline is the **Church of Our Lady of Mount Carmel**. The church was completed in 1958 on the site of a church designed by Cassar that was also badly damaged during World War II. The dome is 73 metres (240ft) high and dominates the spire of **St Paul's Anglican Cathedral**, built on the site of the Auberge d'Allemagne with funds donated by Queen Adelaide, the consort of William IV of the United Kingdom, in 1839.

GRAND HARBOUR SIDE

A number of interesting buildings are situated on the Grand Harbour side of Republic Street. If you enter the city by car you will find yourself facing one of the most beautiful historic buildings of Valletta, the **Auberge de Castille** (no public access). Constructed in 1574, it was home to knights from Castile, Leon and Portugal. Grand Master Emanuel Pinto De Fonseca added the beautifully ornamented Baroque facade in 1744. The *auberge* now serves as the office of the prime minister.

From the *auberge*, head right, past a small Greek revival style building – the Malta Stock Exchange – to **Upper Barrakka Gardens** , once a private garden of the Knights and today offering the most spectacular views of the Grand Harbour. The gardens, laid out in the 17th century, sit on the St Peter and St Paul Bastion. Plaques and sculptures adorn the flowerbeds but most people head to the open terrace, camera in hand. The view is a spectacular panorama stretching from Fort Ricasoli, facing Fort St Elmo at the harbour's entrance on the left, to deep into the harbour's reaches on the right, where the dockyard repairs international shipping. Facing you is Fort St Angelo and the Three Cities. It's from here that you can also hop aboard one of Valletta's most unusual transport services – the Barrakka lift.

Follow St Paul Street alongside Castille until you reach the **Church of St Paul Shipwrecked**. Designed by Gerolamo Cassar, this is one of the oldest churches in Valletta, and has several paintings by Attilio Palombi depicting scenes from the saint's life. A large wooden statue adorns the interior and the church safeguards a jewelled reliquary that contains a relic of the saint's wrist and a piece of the column on which St Paul is believed to have been martyred.

Back on the city wall at the Grand Harbour side (from St Paul's Street walk down several flights of stairs) are **Lower Barrakka Gardens.** They also offer a view across the harbour, but give a different perspective, with a vista of Fort Ricasoli at the mouth of Grand Harbour. In the centre of the gardens is a Doric temple, erected as a memorial to Sir Alexander Ball, who led the blockade that defeated the French in 1800.

Below you is the Siege Bell memorial, unveiled by Queen Elizabeth II during a visit to Malta in 1992. It is dedicated to the men who lost their lives in the 1940–3 wartime convoys. From

⊘ THE BARRAKKA LIFT

One of Valletta's latest additions is the Barrakka Lift, opened in 2012 and reached through the Upper Barrakka Gardens.

This lift originally serviced the city around the 1900s, but eventually fell into disrepair and was closed down. Thankfully, in 2009 funds were secured through the EU to rebuild the lift from scratch. The current lift stands at an impressive 60 metres tall, making it the second-tallest structure in Malta. It's now the ideal mode of transport to connect the cruise terminal and Valletta waterfront to the centre of the capital – and it takes just 25 seconds to travel from bottom to top.

the bell you can clearly see the long plain facade of the **Sacra Infermeria**, once the hospital run by the Knights – one of the most advanced medical facilities of its day when it opened in 1574. The hospital was still in use as a medical facility until after the end of World War I. The huge wards – the longest measured 161m (528ft) – are now home to the **Mediterranean Conference Centre** (www.mcc.com.mt), one of Malta's post-independence success stories, which hosts several major international conferences a year.

OUTSIDE VALLETTA

Valletta does not have a monopoly on history or wonderful architecture. Almost every town or village on the islands will have a building – often a church – that is worthy of note and exploration. The countryside is also littered with military remains. These include forts and towers from the time of the Knights, as well as 19th- and 20th-century fortifications.

FLORIANA

Any trip to Valletta will entail travelling through **Floriana** ❷, situated just outside the gates of the capital. It is named after military engineer Pietro Floriani, who was charged with extending Valletta's defences in the mid-16th century, giving rise to the creation of this suburb. Floriana was rebuilt after World War II, and the finest buildings faithfully recreated.

The gateway marking the entrance to Floriana sits astride two lanes of a main road that bisects the town. Called the **Portes des Bombes**, it was built in 1721 as part of Valletta's outer ring of defence, but has undergone several alterations since then. In the 19th century roads were cut through the bastion walls on either side to speed the flow of traffic.

The dome that dominates the skyline belongs to **St Publius Church**, named after the 'headman' of Malta at the time when the apostle Paul was shipwrecked on the island while on a voyage to Rome (as a prisoner of the Romans) in AD60. Publius invited St Paul to stay in his home, and St Paul is said to have repaid the kindness by healing his father of an illness. He also made Publius one of his first

Malta Experience

Next to the Mediterranean Conference Centre is The Malta Experience (www. themaltaexperience.com; hourly programmes Mon–Fri 11am–4pm, Sat–Sun 11am–2pm), a multi-media spectacular that takes viewers on a 50-minute journey through the history of the islands. It is a great way to get your bearings and an excellent introduction to the sights of Malta.

The Portes des Bombes leads into Floriana

converts to Christianity, and Publius went on to become the first bishop of Malta. The square in front of the church has granary silos beneath it, dating from 1660, which were in continual use until the 1960s. It is now a popular venue for large outdoor concerts, especially during the summer months.

FORT RINELLA

Facing Fort St Elmo across the Grand Harbour is **Fort Ricasoli**, with a beautiful gate, dated 1698. Now in disrepair, film companies use it to build large-scale open-air sets. Both *Gladiator* and *Troy* were filmed here; for *Gladiator* the replica of the Colosseum was built in the large central space.

Further east around the point is **Fort Rinella** (www.fort rinella.com; Mon–Sat 10am–5pm). This 19th-century fort was built to house the largest cannon ever made – a 100-tonne gun that no other fortification could accommodate. The muzzle-loader required a team of 22 to man it in action, and could penetrate 38cm (15ins) of metal at a distance of 8km (5 miles). Military re-enactments here include the firing of howitzers. Next to the fort is the **Mediterranean Film Studios** (www.mediterraneanfilmstudios.com), which opened in 1963. Several major films as well as TV dramas, commercials and music videos have been made at the studios, which have the largest water tank facilities in Europe.

THE THREE CITIES

When the Order of St John took up residence in the Grand Harbour, they settled in Birgu and its suburb, Bormla. A small community lived on the neighbouring promontory, l'Isla. After the Great Siege victory, Birgu became known as Vittoriosa (The Victorious One), Bormla became Cospicua (Conspicuous) and l'Isla (The Island), became Senglea, named after Grand Master Claude de la Sengle, who divided the land for it to be used for dwellings. Although the traffic signs say Vittoriosa, Cospicua and Senglea, many Maltese use the original names: Birgu, Bormla and l'Isla. They were designated cities during the brief French occupation.

The first military action the Knights carried out on arrival was the reinforcement of the old fortification jutting out into the harbour. This they renamed **Fort St Angelo**.

In 1565 this fort withstood repeated Turkish attacks, its defenders consisting of 600 knights and fewer than 1,000 men-at-arms. Reinforced after the victory, the fort has remained unchanged in outline since 1689. The British used it as a naval station and renamed it HMS St Angelo. The Maltese government has leased part of the fort back to the Sovereign Military Order of Malta, so much of the upper bastions are now off limits to visitors. The fort's €14.5-million restoration was completed in 2015 and the complex opened to the public in November 2016 (open daily 9am–5pm).

Vittoriosa

The town of **Vittoriosa** ❸ sits behind the fort. Vittoriosa Square is diminutive but forms a central point for several thoroughfares through the town – the streets are still laid out as they were in medieval times, with bends and curves rather than straight lines. Birgu developed according to the needs of the Knights. Seven *auberges* and a hospital were built here, though these facilities were later transferred to Valletta. A convent beside the hospital still has a community of sisters, more than 400 years later, and a bishop's palace, built in 1542, now serves as a school.

In 1574 another more powerful servant of the church arrived to oversee the deeds of the Knights and the Maltese population: the Inquisitor. He took up offices in what had previously been the Law Courts and embellished the building. The Inquisition remained all-powerful until the French abolished it in 1798. Grand Inquisitors were charged with the responsibility of investigating any evidence of heresy. This they did with ruthless efficiency. They also acted as arbitrators in the case of disputes between the Knights, the Grand Master and the bishop. The plain facade of the **Inquisitor's Palace** (www. heritagemalta.org; daily 9am–5pm) houses plain prison cells and dungeons on the lower floors, which contrast with the highly decorated private apartments of the Inquisitors themselves above, including the Tribunal room where evidence was heard and verdicts were issued.

On the waterfront, with the impressive Cottonera Marina full of sleek yachts and cruisers, and a wealth of good restaurants, stands the **Church of St Lawrence**. The original edifice, dating from 1530, has been embellished over the centuries, including the addition of a Baroque facade. Inside, an altarpiece by Mattia Preti graces one of nine altars. Outside the church is the **Freedom Monument**, with bronze figures depicting the departure of the last British serviceman who stepped on to a naval vessel from this wharf in 1979.

Enter the wharf under the arch at the waterside here. This area was a hive of activity under British rule, as Malta was a major naval and military outpost of the Empire. The British built a large victualling yard and bakery along the wharf to restock the ships and feed the garrison. Following their closure in 1979, the buildings were allowed to fall into decay but part of the bakery has now been refurbished and houses the **National Maritime Museum** (www.heritagemalta.org; daily 9am–5pm). Here you will find displays of artefacts salvaged in Maltese waters, along with naval uniforms and paintings. The tactic textbooks and models of ships on display were used in the training of naval cadets. There is also an interesting section on traditional Maltese craft.

Vittoriosa was protected on the landward side by a wall consisting of a series of bastions and curtains (sheer walls). Three gateways allowed entry and can still be seen. The only remaining gate in use is the pedestrianised **Couvre Port** dating from 1727.

Facing Vittoriosa, also jutting into the harbour, is **Senglea ❹**, named after Grand Master Claude de la Sengle who built its fortifications in 1551. **Safe Haven Garden**, at the very tip, offers beautiful views across the harbour to the Valletta skyline. It is protected by a recreated stone

Statue on Vittoriosa waterfront

vedette atop a bastion, decorated with an eye and an ear to indicate that it is all-seeing and all-hearing.

Today, Senglea is a working city. Most of its population travels to the Malta shipyard at Frenchmen's Creek. The tradition of shipbuilding and repair carries on into modern times, with huge cranes and jacks on the move every day.

Cospicua ❺, between Senglea and Vittoriosa, was the largest of the three cities in the 16th century but was badly damaged in World War II, and was rebuilt as an industrial town.

All three cities were bound together in a huge fortification built in the 1680s when the Grand Master Nicola Cottoner commissioned and paid for a massive outer protective wall in case of another attack. About 3km (2 miles) of wall stretched from the waters of Kalkara Creek (north of Vittoriosa) to Frenchmen's Creek. There were five entry gates; the central one has a bust of Cottoner and beautiful embellishments in

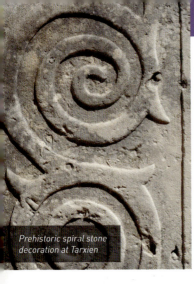

Prehistoric spiral stone decoration at Tarxien

stone. The new walls, which came to be known as the **Cottonera Lines**, can clearly be seen as you travel the area, and are as impressive now as they would have been to a Turkish janissary in the 17th century.

THE HYPOGEUM AND THE TARXIEN TEMPLES

Paola ❻ is a busy town, 10 minutes by car from Valletta. Within its boundaries is a very important ancient site, discovered in the early 19th century. The **Ħal-Saflieni Hypogeum** (www.heritagemalta.org; guided tours only, temporarily closed) began life as a simple cave where Neolithic settlers buried their dead (*hypogeum* is a Greek word meaning underground). Sometime between 3800 and 2500 BC, the population began to cut and shape the cave, creating a second level of chambers, and later a third, until the caves reached 12 metres (40ft) underground. The sheer scale of the hypogeum is astounding, and the workmanship involved is evidence of the sophistication of these ancient peoples. The remains of more than 7,000 people have been found here, and many artefacts excavated are now on display at the National Museum of Archaeology in Valletta (see page 32). The tour starts with a brief introductory exhibition and a multilingual audio-visual film focusing on the temple-building peoples and the Hypogeum's relationship to Malta's temple sites.

In the nearby town of **Tarxien** ❼, crowded by modern sub-urbs, stand the **Tarxien Temples** (www.heritagemalta.org; daily 9am–5pm), which provide an important record of Maltese life in the 4th millennium BC. Pronounced 'Tar-shin', they were discovered in 1915, when a farmer, concerned about the huge stones that littered his fields, called someone in to investigate. Archaeologist Dr Themistocles Zammit excavated the whole site and discovered three temples. The Tarxien Temples show evidence of the great strides made during the temple-building phases by builders whose only tools were axes and flints; trees were used to lever stones into position. The middle temple (3200BC) is more substantial and accurate than earlier ones at Ġgantija on Gozo (see page 79). Libation holes, used to wor-ship the gods of the underworld, can be seen, but the carved stone slabs depicting bulls and pigs are copies; the originals are in Valletta's National Museum of Archaeology.

The town of Tarxien is also interesting; far away from the unlovely suburbs around the temple site, the heart of the old town is charming, its buildings little changed over centuries.

SLIEMA, ST JULIAN'S AND PACEVILLE

These are the holiday destinations for many visitors to the islands. On the shore of Marsamxett Harbour facing Valletta, **Sliema** ❽ was until the 1970s the island's only resort area. But as tourism developed, so St Julian's and Paceville further along the coastline began to take over with an ever-increasing variety of hotels, restaurants, cafés and bars. This is the area that comes to life at night and buzzes until the early hours.

Sliema started out as a sheltered fishing village, but as people began to find Valletta too hot in summer, they built houses in Sliema in order to enjoy the cooler sea air. The village grew into a modern, sophisticated town, and now apartments in blocks that

Shopping

Sliema is Malta's shopping capital. The main shopping avenues are Tower Road, the Strand and Manuel Dimech Street. The Plaza (www.plaza-shopping.com) and Tigne Point (www.the pointmalta.com) are the largest malls. There is little in the way of individual local shops, but it bristles with international high street and designer brands.

line the sea-facing promenade command seriously high prices. There are fine hotels and shops, and from its harbour cruise boats set out for tours around the islands and harbours. There are even disco boats that sail by night.

As more land was required for houses, Sliema expanded to become linked with **St Julian's**, a fishing village further north. Its picturesque bay is now edged with restaurants and St Julian's has become the place to be. Joining St Julian's is **Paceville**, the nightlife centre that never seems to sleep. There are bars, discos, cinemas and a wide variety of restaurants, in all price ranges. On the perimeter is tranquil **St George's Bay**, with some luxurious five-star hotels and beach lidos. Jutting out to sea is the **Dragonara Casino** (www.dragonaracasino.com), with gaming tables in the elegant setting of a summer palazzo once owned by a marquis.

THE SOUTHEAST

The southeastern section of Malta is an interesting mixture of old and new, where tradition carries on alongside 21st-century industry. A number of bays offer shelter for boats, especially Marsaxlokk and Marsascala. This is where you will find the fishing fleets, and some of the best fish restaurants.

Marsaskala is the most easterly town on Malta. Little fishing boats bob on the water of the picturesque narrow bay, and it has developed into a tranquil resort, with simple restaurants and cafés.

MARSAXLOKK

To the south of Marsaskala is **Marsaxlokk** ⑨ ('Mar-sash-lok'), with the largest fishing fleet in Malta. Marsaxlokk Bay is the islands' largest bay, and traditional brightly painted fishing boats such as the *luzzu*, sit on the water or rest on the dockside. You will find fishermen tending to the boats or mending nets, constantly chatting as they work. Fish restaurants have tables by the water where you can enjoy an alfresco lunch or dinner, and there is a daily market here with table linens and lace for sale.

If you head towards the lighthouse and fort at Delimara Point, you will pass the Carmelite church of **Tas-Silġ**, a site of religious worship for centuries before the birth of Christ. Unfortunately, this area has been visually spoiled by a power station.

GĦAR DALAM

On the edge of Birżebbuġa is the fascinating cave system of **Għar Dalam** with a small **museum** (www.heritagemalta.org; daily

The Eye of Osiris painted on a boat

9am–5pm) that displays finds from the site. The cave runs for 144 metres (472ft) into the limestone rock and its fissures link to caves in the west that once formed part of an ancient watercourse. During the Pleistocene period this area was a haven for hippopotami, dwarf elephants, micro-mammals and birds, whose remains were fossilised over hundreds of thousands of years. The bones indicate that Malta was once rich in water and vegetation and joined to what is now the European mainland. Above the pebble layer is the so-called 'deer' layer, dated to approximately 18,000 years ago. The top, or 'cultural layer', dates to less than 10,000 years ago and holds evidence of the first humans on the island. The museum displays thousands of specimens in glass cases.

The Eye of Osiris

All traditional brightly coloured fishing boats in Maltese waters have an eye painted on both sides of their bow, to ward off any evil that may be out at sea. Osiris was the Egyptian god of fertility, the underworld and the dead. Here he wards off evil in the company of saints, as most boats are named after saints and carry little shrines. Every spring, before fishermen put their boats on the water, they paint the eye afresh for maximum protection.

Birżebbuġia (bir-zeb-boo-ja) has some tourist infrastructure. However, the building of a modern container port nearby has blighted its best beach at Pretty Bay. Malta is the perfect central depot for container traffic in the Mediterranean and the Malta Freeport tranships goods and oil from all corners of the world.

Malta International Airport (www.maltairport.com) cuts a swathe across this southeastern area. **Żurrieq** is the largest of the small villages that lie on the far side of the airfield. It has a pretty church dedicated to St Catherine (1659). Inside is an attractive altarpiece by Mattia Preti, who also decorated St John's Co-Cathedral in Valletta.

BLUE GROTTO

Follow the coast road and you come to picturesque **Wied-iż-Żurrieq**, a fjordlike inlet in the dramatic coastline where there is a tiny fishing village used by a handful of fishermen

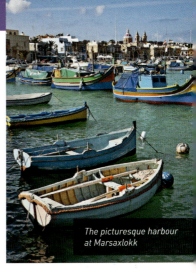

The picturesque harbour at Marsaxlokk

whose colourful boats you will see bobbing in the water or pulled up on the steep hillside for repair. A number of small craft leave the narrow concrete slip that acts as a jetty for tours to the **Blue Grotto** ❿ (www.bluegrottomalta.com.mt; daily 9am–5pm, winter until 3.30pm, weather permitting; regular 30-minute trips) and the rugged coastline. The best time to see the grotto is early in the day before the sun gets too high. Because it is so appealing, Wied-iż-Żurrieq is a popular destination for tour groups who flock into the simple cafés for refreshments and souvenirs.

ĦAĠAR QIM AND MNAJDRA

A short distance away on the road leading along the cliffs are the spectacular Neolithic remains of **Ħaġar Qim** and **Mnajdra** ⓫ (www.heritagemalta.org; daily Apr–Sept 9am–6pm, Oct–Mar 9am–5pm), on a hillside overlooking the tiny island of **Filfla**.

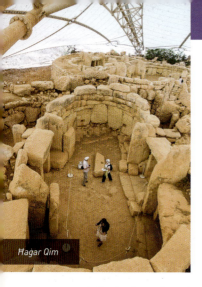
Ħaġar Qim

The visitor centre has lots of interesting information. The island is a bird sanctuary and is home to a unique species of lizard. Ħaġar Qim, which sits atop the cliffs, was discovered as early as 1839 and consists of a series of temples. Unfortunately it was constructed of soft stone and has weathered considerably. A number of 'fat lady' statuettes were found here, indicating its use as a fertility shrine, and there are even tethering loops for animals in the stone, but no one is sure if these were used for sacrifice. The 'fat ladies' are on display in the National Museum of Archaeology in Valletta.

Mnajdra ('Im-naydra') sits below Ħaġar Qim, around 500 metres (546yds) down a steep path. It is made up of two main temples dating from around 3400BC and is probably the best-preserved site on Malta. Its doorways are particularly fine, with posts and lintels. It is worthwhile climbing the slope behind the temples – from here you can get an overview of the whole site and can appreciate its size and complicated structure.

HEADING INLAND

If you are travelling from Valletta towards Mdina, you will see the remains of the **Wignacourt Aqueduct**, which began to supply water to Valletta in 1610.

Turn into **Balzan** to find **San Anton Palace and Gardens** ⓬, built during the late 1620s as a summer palace for Grand Master Antoine de Paule, who personally supervised the layout of the formal gardens that surround it. Subsequent grand masters added to the palace itself and the British contributed the veranda beneath the turret. Filled with paintings and fine art, the palace is now the official residence of the president of Malta and is closed to visitors. The beautifully kept **gardens** (daily June–Oct 7am–6pm, Nov–May 7am–5pm; free) contain palms, cypress, jacarandas, araucarias and other exotic plants, some more than three centuries old, together with graceful fountains, pools, statues and colourful flowerbeds. In addition there are glasshouses sheltering indoor plants, and an aviary. Various flower and animal shows are held here throughout the year.

The main road continues to Mdina – you can see its walls and spires dominating the horizon. After a couple of minutes you will see a turning to the right, leading to **Ta' Qali Craft Village**,

⊘ VILLA BOLOGNA

Located a couple of corners away from San Anton Palace and Gardens is one of Malta's most breathtaking stately homes. **Villa Bologna** (www.villabologna.com; Mon–Fri 9am–5pm, Sat 9am–1pm) was built in 1745 by one of Grand Master Pinto's senior advisors as a wedding gift to his daughter. Its gardens are one of the finest examples of a historic Maltese garden and have just been renovated giving them a new lease of life. The estate also hosts one of the best potteries on the island, which was relocated here after the original one in Ta' Qali was destroyed during World War II. The pottery produces thousands of hand-made pieces a year, which make great souvenirs.

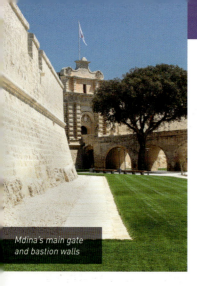
Mdina's main gate and bastion walls

near the National Sports Stadium. Ta' Qali has a number of artisans working in what was formerly an air base. You will see lace-making, glass-blowing and potting, and be able to buy straight from the manufacturer. It is gradually being turned into an attractive craft village.

MDINA

Finally, the walls of **Mdina** ⑬ loom large ahead. The Phoenicians called the town Maleth, and it was known in Roman times as Melita. In the 9th century, the Aghlabids transformed Mdina into a fortified citadel, building impregnable walls to protect it from enemy raids. Mdina (literally 'the walled city') was the capital of the island until the Knights of St John arrived in 1530 and made their headquarters at Grand Harbour; from then on it was simply referred to as Città Vecchia (Old City).

During the Great Siege of 1565 the Turks concentrated their efforts on the Grand Harbour, giving the cavalry garrison at Mdina numerous opportunities for sorties that gradually wore down the enemy. Mdina also deterred the enemy by reinforcing the battlements with women disguised as soldiers – a ruse that completely deceived the Turks. Although Mdina lost its prestige as the island's capital under the Knights, it later became the bishops' See, and was also allowed to remain the seat of the Università, the government advisory body made up of patricians and the clergy.

The city was badly damaged in an earthquake in 1693. It was not until the 1720s that work began to rebuild and include some open spaces for the population to enjoy. While the street plan remains essentially medieval, with several fine period palaces, many of the public buildings date from the period of post-disaster Baroque building. Just below the outside walls, you'll also find the gardens in the ditch beneath the bastions, which is perfect for a quiet walk.

Magisterial Palace

When you step through the main gate of Mdina you step back in time – no neon signs or fast-food joints, no visitors' traffic. You can spend time wandering along the narrow alleys and the city walls – it takes only a few minutes to stroll the 400m (1300ft) length of the main street.

Just inside the main gate you will see the Magisterial Palace on your right. Built by Grand Master Manoel de Vilhena in the 1720s in French Baroque style, it was used as the seat of the commune – the local administrative assembly. The palace now houses the **National Museum of Natural History** Ⓐ (www.heritagemalta.org; daily 9am–5pm), with its collections of fossils, flora and fauna, and diagrams that explain the geology of the islands. Attached to the palace are buildings that once housed the law courts, and beneath them are dungeons.

At the **Mdina Dungeons** (www.dungeonsmalta.com; daily 10am–4.30pm) exhibit

Città Nobile

King Alphonse of Aragon conferred the title of Città Nobile on Mdina in 1428 after the city heroically withstood an attack by Islamic corsairs. Three thousand of the island's inhabitants were taken prisoner in the raid.

you will see multifarious gory methods used to extract confessions, including the favoured forms of torture, in the actual buildings where they took place. The scenes of disfigurement and amputation are rather realistic, especially in conjunction with the spine-chilling sound effects, so it may not be suitable for young children.

Villegaignon Street

Many of the main attractions can be found on **Villegaignon Street**, which cuts through the heart of the town. As you turn into this street, on your left is **Casa Inguanez**, the palace of the oldest noble family on Malta. Across the narrow street the **Chapel of St Agatha** is dedicated to the Christian martyr who came to Malta to escape Roman persecution in the 3rd century. The church dates from 1471 and was redesigned in 1694.

You will find several suitably costumed women offering fliers for attractions as you walk down the street. Even in an area as small as Mdina there are several audio-visual walk-through attractions vying for your attention. Down the narrow alleyway of Mesquita Street you can find **The Mdina Experience** (www.themdinaexperience.com; daily 10am–5pm), and on the old ramparts on Magazine Street is **The Knights of Malta** (www.theknightsofmalta.com; daily 10am–5pm), which concentrates on the Order, its history and its role on the island.

Cathedral

The main square in the citadel is flanked on the western side by the **Cathedral of St Paul** Ⓑ (Mon–Fri 9.30am–4.30pm, Sat 9.30am–3.30pm), said to have been built on the site where St Paul converted Publius, then the headman of the community, to Christianity in AD 60. A church has existed on the site since the 4th century. This was enlarged under Count Roger's rule in 1090 and extended again in 1490. Following the earthquake of 1693 it was completely redesigned, although some features, such as the back arch of the church, and an Irish bogwood door dating from AD 900, remain. The work was undertaken by Maltese architect Lorenzo Gafà and is a masterpiece, with columns, twin bell towers and a fine dome. Inside you will find a marble font dating from 1495, and a beautiful pavement of marble tombstones commemorating religious dignitaries. The painting by Mattia Preti depicting St Paul riding on a white charger recalls the time during the Saracen attack of 1494 when it is said that St Paul, mounted on a horse, appeared on the battlements of Mdina to frighten away the invaders.

Across the small square outside the south door of the cathedral is the old **Seminary**. The main entrance of this majestic

Aerial view of Mdina

Baroque building, which dates from 1729, is flanked by two stone giants supporting an ornate stone balcony. Since 1968, the buildings have been used to house the **Cathedral Museum** (Mon–Sat 9.30am–4.30pm and Sat 9.30am–3.30pm, a combined ticket allows entry to the cathedral and museum), which has a wide-ranging collection of religious artefacts and painting, including several medieval manuscripts and papal bulls relating to Malta, as well as engravings by Rembrandt and woodcuts by Durer. The museum also features an impressive numismatic collection that includes Maltese coins ranging from Carthaginian times to the present day.

From the cathedral, carry on along Villegaignon Street. You will be walking towards the corner statue of the Madonna and Child on the left, which adorns the **Carmelite Church**.

The domed ceiling of the Cathedral of St Paul

Anti-French riots began here in 1798 when the French commandant, Masson, indicated that he was going to plunder the treasury of the church.

Located right in the heart of Mdina, the **Carmelite Priory** C (www.carmelitepriory.org; Tue–Sat 10am–4pm, guided tours only, pre-booking essential) offers insight into the lives of the Carmelite friars who reside here, with information about the spiritual and the daily way of life of their predecessors in this spectacular 17th-century priory. Stunning highlights include the decorative refectory, an authentic kitchen, a typical friar's cell and an oratory.

Palazzo Falson

Opposite the church, just a little further along the street, is **Palazzo Falson** D, also known as Norman House because of the shape of its windows. Now a museum (www.palazzofalson. com; Tue–Sun 10am–4pm), with many items bequeathed by the house's philanthropic former resident, Palazzo Falson was begun in 1283. Following the expulsion of the Jewish population from Malta in 1492, the synagogue that stood next to the house fell into disuse and was bought by the Falson family. The present house was built in 1495, using the extra space. The stone walls and inner courtyard have changed little since that time. Paintings, furniture and other everyday articles demonstrate family life played out over the centuries.

A little way beyond the palazzo are the walls of the citadel at **Bastion Square**, offering fine views across nearby valleys towards Mosta. You can walk around the walls here, or visit the cafés. Make your way round to Magazines Street where you will find the **Greek Gate**, a less-used entrance to the city than the main gate, but a considerably older one. Part of the bastion dates from the period of Arab rule.

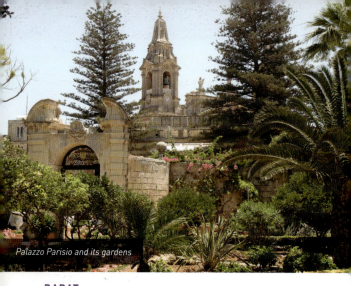
Palazzo Parisio and its gardens

RABAT

Beyond the walls of Mdina, **Rabat** could not be more of a contrast. Rabat (an Arab word meaning village) began to grow outside Mdina's walls as a residential suburb that would serve the city during the period of Arab rule. Today, with no Arab traces, it is an untidy town with narrow streets. Dominating its centre is the parish church of **St Paul** (1691) with a **grotto** (daily 9.30am–4pm) beneath that is said to have miraculous powers and is consequently a place of pilgrimage. Legend has it that St Paul lived here for three months in stark simplicity. In 1748, to honour the saint, Grand Master Pinto donated the statue that stands here. Pope John Paul II visited the grotto in May 1990.

The grotto is linked to the **Wignacourt Collegiate Museum** (www.wignacourtmuseum.com; daily 9.30am–4pm), a charming old palazzo that used to be a pilgrims' hostel. The museum has a varied collection of paintings by renowned artists, including Mattia Preti. The Wignacourt Museum has become a cultural centre, often offering space to established and up-and-coming artists to display their art, and hosting a series of cultural events in the summer called Summer Under the Stars. Apart from St Paul's Grotto, the museum is also connected to a part of St Paul's Catacombs Complex (see page 63), and war shelters dating back to the World War II.

Nearby are the Catacombs of St Cataldus, St Paul and St Agatha. These macabre underground burial places were dug into the stone by early Christians who, in times of religious intolerance, often conducted their religious services in the chambers. **St Cataldus** was dug at the end of the 2nd century while **St Paul's Catacombs 🄴** (www.heritagemalta.org; daily 9am–4.30pm) were built after AD 400. More than 1,000 people were buried here. **St Agatha's Catacombs** (http://stagatha malta.com/catacombs.html; daily 9am–4.30pm) are reached through a crypt. It has chambers decorated with frescoes dating from the 12th century and a pleasant small museum.

Just outside the walls of Mdina near the Greek Gate is one of the few remains of the islands' Roman period, a villa believed to have belonged to a wealthy merchant. Reconstructed from the foundations up, it is now the **Domus Romana** (daily 9am–4.30pm), a museum of Roman antiquities with a number of interesting mosaics and a collection of Roman objects found here and elsewhere in Malta, including marble statues and busts, terracotta ornaments, glassware and pottery, and some amphorae.

MOSTA

Only 3km (2 miles) northeast of Mdina is **Mosta 🄳**, whose major attraction can be seen from the walls of the old capital. The

Rotunda of the Church of Santa Maria Assunta (http://mosta church.com; free) is said to have the fourth largest dome in Europe and is a masterpiece of design and construction, built without interior scaffolding. It was designed by George Grognet de Vasse, a Maltese engineer of French origin, and is based on the Pantheon in Rome. Its 51m (167ft) high dome is 45m (147ft) in diameter with walls 6m (19ft) thick. During World War II, a German bomb pierced the dome and fell into the church below. The fact that it did not explode was attributed to the intervention of the Virgin Mary. A replica of the bomb is on display in the sacristy.

It is worth taking time to explore Mosta's medieval alleys and streets. Two kilometres (1 mile) northeast is the city of **Naxxar** ⑮ (see box).

VICTORIA LINES

To the southwest of Mosta and Mdina, Malta becomes more rural, with only a few farming settlements surrounded by terraced fields and joined by bumpy roads. You will see vestiges of old fortifications, including a defensive wall running across the centre of the island, originally built by the British during the Victorian period

◉ NAXXAR AND PALAZZO PARISIO

Naxxar is a picturesque city with a beautiful church and attractive village square. One of the best reasons to visit is easily missed but well-worth seeking out – the magnificent Palazzo Parisio (www.palazzoparisio.com; daily 9am–6pm; charge). This historic stately home is family run, and incorporates glorious staterooms, two good restaurants, a wonderful garden and a gift shop.

to protect the south of the island should it be attacked from the north. The **Victoria Lines**, as they are known, became something of a white elephant when warfare changed in the 20th century. Onwards towards the village of **Mġarr** are more Neolithic remains at **Ta' Ħaġrat and Skorba** (Tue, Thu and Sat 9am–4.30pm), another of Malta's Unesco world heritage sites.

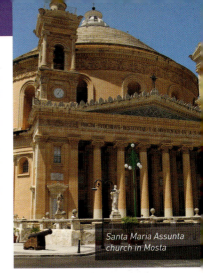
Santa Maria Assunta church in Mosta

BUSKETT GARDENS

South of Rabat, the main road leads down towards the coast. **Verdala Castle** 🔟, on this road, was originally a summer residence for Grand Master de Verdale. Designed by Gerolamo Cassar in 1586, the building was intended to look like a fortified castle – complete with dry moat – even though it was never meant to withstand an attack. Today the castle is the summer residence of the president and only rarely open to the public. The extensive grounds are split into two sections, those which form the private gardens of the palace, and an area of natural woodland beyond, known as the Boschetto or **Buskett Gardens**, which was once a hunting area, alive with game, and now a favourite picnic place for Maltese families at weekends during the summer. A large horticultural show is held here each year on 29 June, the feast day of saints Peter and Paul.

The road from Rabat stops abruptly at **Dingli Cliffs**, named after a nearby village. The precipitous drops along much of the south coast are awe-inspiring and are at their most spectacular around Dingli. There are several walking trails in the area; east to the pretty, secluded cove of **Għar Lapsi**, or west to the highest point on Malta at 253 metres (820ft) above sea level, marked by the **Madalena Chapel**.

THE NORTHWEST

The northwest of Malta has traditionally been less populated than the southeast. In this region you will find far more farming, much more open space, and resorts that are different in character to those in the Sliema–St Julian's area. At the furthest point is **Ċirkewwa**, with a regular ferry service to Gozo and day trip boats to Comino.

At **Baħar iċ-Ċagħaq** ⑰ you will find two attractions to please children. The **Splash and Fun Water Park** (www.splashand fun.com.mt; 24 June–9 Sept daily 9am–9pm, 19 May–23 June and 10 Sept–7 Oct daily 9am–6pm) has slides, pools and funfair rides, Next door to it is **Mediterraneo Marine Park** (www. mediterraneopark.com; open daily) with sea lions and dolphins that perform daily, and an opportunity to swim with the dolphins. The Marine Park operates education programmes, which involve getting behind the scenes with the trainers and park workers who keep the animals healthy and happy. These sessions are open to the public and last for 90 minutes.

QAWRA

The road continues round the coast to **Salina Bay** ⑱, named for the salt flats that have been used for centuries to produce this most important of minerals. Salina Bay marks the start of the second major area developed for tourists, which stretches around the headland of **Qawra**. This area is characterised by

Buġibba overlooks St Paul's Bay

more self-catering accommodation and fewer large hotels than in Sliema–St Julian's. The nightlife is a bit more raucous and a little less sophisticated. Having said that, there are more than enough bars, clubs and eateries to satisfy the thousands who enjoy coming here every year. It is also the setting for Malta's **National Aquarium** (www.aquarium.com.mt; Sun–Fri 10am–6pm, Sat until 8pm), which opened in 2013 – perfect for family days out.

BUĠIBBA AND ST PAUL'S BAY

As you travel further round the headland, Qawra melds into **Buġibba** (Boo-jib-ba), a modern town overlooking the waters of **St Paul's Bay** ⑲. On the far side of the bay is St Paul's Island, where the saint is believed to have been shipwrecked. His statue dominates the barren rock. Both Buġibba and Qawra have a wide selection of hotels and self-catering apartments, and from the Buġibba waterfront day trip boats take visitors north to Gozo and Comino or south to Valletta. Just inland from Buġibba, in the small town of **Burmarrad**, is the simple church of **San Pawl Milqi** (St Paul Welcomed), said to be the site where he first preached to the Maltese people.

GĦAJN TUFFIEĦA

Two of the islands' most picturesque sandy beaches are **Għajn Tuffieħa** 20 (ʿAyn tuff-eer-ha') and **Golden Bay**, set among dramatic cliffs and separated by a tiny tower that was once a watchtower of the Knights. Golden Bay is the larger of the two, with a car park close to the extensive beach facilities at the water's edge. Għajn Tuffieħa can be reached only by a climb down a long stretch of steps or down a rough path, so even in the height of summer it is the less crowded of the two. Għajn Tuffieħa has only a small café to offer refreshments. Both beaches are ideal for children.

Not far from these two bays, at the crossroads leading to the first car park, is a signpost to the village of **Mġarr** and to Ġnejna Bay. Mġarr is a farming community, a small village with a tall church dedicated to Santa Marija – it is known as the Egg Church because villagers financed it by donating money generated by selling eggs. Drive through the village, or walk, as the bus (No. 44 from Valletta) does not go any further, and the road runs for about 1km (0.5 miles) through countryside before dipping down into a long fertile valley at the end of which is another sandy beach at **Ġnejna Bay**. The sand here is a little coarse but it is a pretty, if sometimes busy, beach with simple but pleasant facilities. To one side, cut into the rock, is a line of boathouses, used for picnics.

The main road around St Paul's Bay begins to climb up away from the coast, cutting across the verdant **Mistra Valley**, with its tiny beach. At the top of the hill is a turning to **Selmun**, once the location of the Knights' Palace. At the crest of the hill, overlooking the bay, is **Mellieħa**, once a remote defensive settlement but now a busy destination. Signs here also lead to **Anchor Bay**, a beautiful natural cove, great for diving and swimming. Here you will find **Popeye Village** (www.popeye malta.com; daily 9.30am–4.30pm, extended summer hours), originally built in 1980 as a set for the film *Popeye* starring Robin Williams. It's a fun place for children to explore and has an amusement park.

MELLIEĦA BAY

Mellieħa Bay ㉑ tends to get busy in the summer because of **Għadira**, which is probably the best sandy beach on Malta. There are plenty of facilities here if you want to stay for the day, or you could bring a picnic. Behind the beach is a protected area of wetland known as the **Għadira Nature Reserve** (Nov–May Sat–Sun 10.30am–4.30pm; free), an important haven for breeding birds, both

Għadira beach in Mellieħa Bay

native and migratory. It is closed in summer, which is the breeding season.

From Mellieħa Bay it is only a short ride up and over **Marfa Ridge** to Ċirkewwa and the brief ferry crossing to Gozo. Boats also take visitors from the quay for day trips to Comino and the Blue Lagoon. At the top of Marfa Ridge there are junctions with secondary roads that lead left and right along the ridge. Both offer excellent panoramic views of Malta and across to Comino and Gozo. On your left on the hill's crest you'll see the **Red Tower** 50 metres (54yds) from the main road, constructed in 1647; it acted as a post for communications with the Knights' garrison on Gozo. To your right are Armier and Little Armier, two small sandy beaches ideal for young families.

Views across the Comino Channel are beautiful, with the domes of the churches of Gozo clearly visible on the skyline across the straits. Maltese families have small chalets by the sea where they come to enjoy summer weekends.

GOZO

Gozo (Għawdex to the Maltese) is Malta's smaller sibling, and at 67 sq km (26 sq miles), is less than a quarter of the size. Its history mirrors that of its neighbour yet it has a different character. Life moves more slowly here and seems less affected by tourism. Gozo has far fewer visitors – there are fewer than 10 major hotels here – and much more land is given over to farming. It is hillier than Malta, and much greener. Gozo still retains more of its traditional lifestyle, making the island a pleasure to visit. It is great for cycling and hiking, and it was even named the third best diving destination in the world by *Diving Magazine* (April 2013).

Gozo is not immune to development, but most new buildings are constructed of sandstone (the same stone used in the numerous forts and towers), which weathers beautifully and looks wonderful in the mellowing sunlight. Many Gozitans (as the people of Gozo are called) emigrated in the years after World War II and some are now returning to enjoy their old age in the place of their birth. You will see houses with names such as Waltzing Matilda or Stars and Stripes – a sure sign of fond memories of adopted countries far away.

MĠARR

Your first real view of Gozo will be the port of **Mġarr** ㉒ ('Im-jar'), whose buildings extend down a hillside and around a small creek. The commercial ferry port with its fishing boats is more functional than pretty. There is a tourist information office and a bank here, along with a couple of cafés and the ferry

View of Mġarr's port on Gozo

terminal. Beyond the ferry port is a delightful fishing harbour that doubles as a yacht harbour in the season. There are some excellent restaurants here, too, with fresh fish on the menu.

Clearly visible from the ferry as it enters port is the **Church of Our Lady of Lourdes**, perched above the harbour. From the parvis there are excellent views of the channel.

You have to climb up and out of the harbour to go anywhere on Gozo. For cyclists this is an early challenge. All bus routes from the harbour go to Victoria, Gozo's capital. On the way there, just up from the harbour, the road passes through the village of **Ghajnsielem**. In the central square is a monument to Anglu Grech, a local farmer, who, according to tradition, had a vision from the Blessed Virgin Mary requesting him to build a church here. The resulting **Church of Our Lady of Loreto** was completed in 1820.

Nearby at **Xewkija** (Shew-kiya) there is a beautiful church. Its dome, which can be seen quite easily from the main road, is larger than that in Mosta, reputedly making it the third largest unsupported dome in Europe. Dedicated to **St John the Baptist**, the rotunda was built as a replacement for an older church on the site. It was made possible thanks to donations from local people; although begun in 1951, the church was not

St John the Baptist church in Xewkija

consecrated for more than 25 years.

VICTORIA

Situated at the heart of the island, **Victoria** ㉓ is the administrative, business and social hub of Gozo. The town has only been called Victoria since 1897, when the British renamed it in honour of Queen Victoria's Silver Jubilee. You will find that Gozitans refer to it as **Rabat**, its original name.

Saints and fiestas

Victoria is made up of two parishes: St George and St Mary's. There is keen rivalry between the two as they vie to throw the best *festas* with the loudest, most spectacular fireworks. Even their band clubs compete, presenting Verdi and Puccini operas with international singers in the principal roles.

The main thoroughfare through town, Republic Street, leads to **It-Tokk Square** (now officially known as Independence Square) with cafés and a daily morning market. At the west end of the square is the tourist information office, housed in a circular building dating from 1733, which was the **Banco Guiratale**. The old town, just off of It-Tokk, is a maze of narrow alleys where you can find women making lace in the shade of their doorways. There are also numerous craft and antique shops, and a special quarter for old metal kitchenware and other collectibles. Alongside It-Tokk is St George's Square with the **Basilica of St George**. Built in the 1670s and badly damaged in the earthquake of 1693, it is richly decorated, with ceilings painted by the Italian artist Giovanni Battista Conti. The ornate wooden statue of the patron saint was carved in 1841. This is carried through the streets on the saint's day (the third Sunday in July). A painting by Mattia Preti over the choir altar depicts the knight poised at the moment of his victory over the dragon. Also in the area is

St Mary's Cathedral

the **Heart of Gozo Museum** (www.heartofgozo.org.mt; Mon–Sun 9am–5pm; free), opened in 2013, which displays a rich collection of historical and artistic artefacts previously inaccessible to the general public.

The Citadel

Dominating the capital is the **Citadel**, perched on the top of the high ground overlooking the city. This is much smaller than Mdina's, but was created at the same time, in the 9th century, when Aghlabid rulers built the imposing defensive walls. The whole settlement suffered badly during Ottoman raids in 1551 and in the earthquake of 1693. Although the church and a number of administrative buildings were reconstructed, much of the Citadel still lies in ruins. This tiny community has a peaceful atmosphere, especially if you find it empty (try to see it early in the morning or after sunset). The most imposing building is **St Mary's Cathedral** (daily 5am–8pm, no visits during mass), erected soon after the earthquake and designed by Lorenzo Gafà, who also designed St Paul's in Mdina. Unfortunately there was not enough money available to finish the cathedral and a proposed dome was never erected. However, in 1739 the Italian artist Antonio Manuele was commissioned to paint a marvellous *trompe l'oeil* on the ceiling of the church, creating the wonderfully realistic effect of a dome when viewed from the church's nave.

The **Cathedral Museum** (www.gozocathedral.org; Mon–Sat 8.30am–4pm) is accessed through a door at the side of the building. Here you will find gold and silver items that comprise the cathedral treasury, along with vestments, prayer books and other ecclesiastical artefacts. St Mary's feast day is the 15 August, the Assumption, when the statue of Our Lady is carried through the Citadel's crowded streets.

Two important administrative buildings flank the square in front of the cathedral. On the left are the old **Law Courts** (rebuilt in 1687), which link with the Governor's Palace (rebuilt early 1600s). Look for the shield of Grand Master Wignacourt on the facade; he was head of the Order when this building opened.

The arch to your left leads to Bondi's Palace, once the meeting place of the Gozo commune or council. The building dates from the 17th century and now houses **Gozo Archaeological Museum** (www.heritagemalta.org; daily 9am–5pm). The museum has an excellent collection of artefacts from many different eras of the islands' history, including a number of female figurines found at the Neolithic sites. Nearby is a craft area, and you can climb on to the bastions via stone stairs to the right of the museum. To the left you can see the original main gate to the Citadel.

A number of old houses in the Citadel have been restored. The finest is the **Folklore Museum** (www.heritagemalta.org; daily 9am–4.30pm), on Milite Bernardo Street, to the right of the cathedral. Exhibits depict the traditional Gozitan lifestyle, with original farm machinery, weaving looms, and lacemaking paraphernalia. The building itself is fascinating, with stone staircases, narrow corridors and cool stone walls. Look out, too, for the **Gozo Nature Museum** (www.heritagemalta.org; daily 9am–4pm), with a collection of rocks and fossils. The **Armoury** (once the Citadel's granary) has a good collection of old armaments.

The countryside of Gozo offers many attractions, and acres of natural beauty. West of Victoria is the traditional village of **Gharb** (the name means 'west' in Arabic and is pronounced Arb) but before you reach the village, turn off left towards the village of **San Lawrenz**. The parish church has a dome painted a warm red, reminiscent of buildings in Italian and Greek settlements.

DWEJRA

The main road leads on towards the coastline. On the left is **Ta'Dbeigi Craft Village** where you can see lace being made and pottery being painted. It is also home to the workshop of **Gozo Glass** (www.gozoglass.com). The craftsmen are at work here every day, so you can watch pieces being blown, as pigment is added to produce their characteristic vivid hues. Finally, you reach **Dwejra** 24 on the west coast, where there are three remarkable natural attractions.

In a dramatic landscape caused centuries ago by a series of geological faults, the most spectacular sight of all is probably the **Azure Window** (daylight hours; free), a giant stone archway that stands with one foot in the deep, dark-blue sea. The window has featured in several famous film and television productions, such as *Game of Thrones* and the *Clash of the Titans*. Nearby is

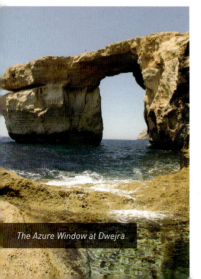
The Azure Window at Dwejra

the **Inland Sea**, a crater filled with seawater that pours in through a concealed fissure in the rocky hillside. Small craft are moored here and there are simple boathouses and a café. Although it is possible to swim, most visitors take a boat trip through the narrow tunnel to the dark-blue sea outside for spectacular views of the Azure

Tip

Buy a combined Discover Gozo ticket (http://shop.heritagemalta.org) at a cost €13 at the time of writing, to save on entrance fees to the most interesting archaeological sites and museums on the island.

Window and the towering cliffs that edge this coastline (negotiate a price with the boatman first). Around the Azure Window are some excellent dive sites.

In the bay on the far left, below a watchtower built by the Knights in 1561 to guard the coastline, is **Dwejra Bay**, with **Fungus Rock** standing at the entrance. In the time of the Knights this rock was reputed to have a rare medicinal plant growing on the top, so a sentry was stationed on the mainland to prevent poachers. It has since been proved that the plant is a fungus with no known medicinal powers.

TA' PINU

Travelling back along the main road to Victoria you will see a turning to the national shrine of **Ta' Pinu** 25 (www.tapinu.org; Mon–Sat 9.30am–4.30pm; free) on your left. This spectacular church, consecrated in 1931, was built on the site of a much older chapel from the 16th century. Ta' Pinu has a fascinating story. In 1883 Carmela Grima, a local woman, came to the old chapel. She heard a voice telling her to pray, yet she was alone in the building. A friend confided that he, too, had heard the voice, and together they prayed for his critically ill mother, who recovered. Following this, several people who came to pray here claimed miracle cures, and gradually the church became a place of pilgrimage. In 1920 work started on this larger church to accommodate the increasing number of devotees visiting it. The original chapel has been incorporated behind the main altar. In a narrow corridor to the side are crutches, splints and baby clothes, all bearing witness to apparent miracle cures after prayer here. Beyond Ta' Pinu across the valley you will see the lighthouse at **Ġordan**, set on a mound offering fine views of the west of the island.

MARSALFORN

On the coast north from Victoria is **Marsalforn** 26, the most developed resort on the island. The collection of small hotels and bars around the narrow bay is lively in summer, although not to the same extent as the resorts on Malta. There is a promenade around the bay where local families come to stroll in the sea air, escaping the heat of their inland villages.

XLENDI

South of Victoria, the coast has only one settlement: the beautiful site of **Xlendi** 27 ('Shlen-dee'), set in a narrow *wied*, or valley, with a sheltered harbour and fleet of small fishing boats bobbing on the calm water. The once tiny community has swelled and modern sandstone apartment blocks now fill the valley, but this has not yet spoiled Xlendi's beauty. There are several fine restaurants here, making it a favourite place for lunch or dinner. You can then sit and admire the view or take to the hills along the footpaths radiating out along the cliffs.

Further east along the cliffs is **Ta'Ċenċ** ('Ta-chench'), which has a superb five-star hotel and numerous fine houses. The land here has ancient dolmen and burial mounds to explore.

Xlendi Bay

At the water's edge is **Mġarr Ix-Xini** ('Im-jar-ish eeni'), with a pretty pebble beach and tiny fish restaurant. The valley is set in a dramatic rural landscape.

ĠGANTIJA

Northeast of Victoria is the town of **Xagħra** ㉖ ('Sha-ra'), set on one of the hills that dot the Gozitan landscape. There are good views of the surrounding area, which may be one of the reasons why it was chosen as the site of a temple during Neolithic times. This is **Ġgantija** (daily 9am–5pm, until 6pm in summer), on the outskirts of the town, the earliest of the four major temple complexes found in Malta.

Ġgantija means 'giant woman', and the huge stones of these two temples are said to have been set in place by such a woman around 3500BC. The site was excavated in the 1820s, and a range of statuary and pottery was discovered and is now displayed in the archaeology museums in Victoria and Valletta. The structure was revealed to be an inner wall of limestone and an outer wall of coralline, a harder rock. Each unit has two pairs of apses. In the inner apse there is a niche with a stone altar. The two temples have a common forecourt where it is thought the congregation would have gathered for worship.

Xagħra has other attractions to offer. It is situated on top of a porous limestone ridge and the whole area is cut with caves and ancient underground watercourses, two of which are open to the public. Both **Ninu's Cave** and **Xerri's Grotto** have stalactites and stalagmites and both lie beneath family homes. You will have a family member as a guide to take you down narrow steps into the caves beneath.

RAMLA BAY

Beyond Xagħra, on the north east coast is **Ramla Bay** ㉙, the only wide sandy beach on Gozo – in fact *ramla* means sand in Maltese. Not surprisingly, it can become busy. You can explore the remains of a small Roman structure just off the beach, and there are footpaths in the hills around. One path leads to Calypso's Cave, said to be the site in Homer's *Odyssey* where Ulysses was held captive by the nymph Calypso. The walk up to the cave is easy and the views impressive.

The high ground in this part of Gozo is topped by

Peaceful coves

East of Ramla Bay there are some beautiful, peaceful coves. Both San Blas Bay and Daħlet Qorrot take a little effort to reach but they are well signposted. San Blas is the island's prettiest sandy beach, reached along the hillside path. Daħlet Qorrot has a much smaller strip of sand, ringed with boathouses.

the fast-growing town of **Nadur**, which is known for its Carnival parade, held on the Sunday before Lent, when local people dress in grotesque masks and bizarre costumes and generally make mischief. Many of the modern houses here have been built for expatriates from countries around the world. They spare no expense in creating the most beautiful facades; the ornate balconies and columns are a fitting continuation of traditional Gozitan building techniques.

The rocks of Ggantija Temple

COMINO

The nearest most people get to tiny **Comino** (2.7 sq km/1 sq mile in total) is gazing at it from the deck of the ferry to Gozo. The island has a permanent population of only six, no vehicles are permitted, and there is just one small hotel. Comino is thus a great place to get away from it all, for walking and relaxing. The most famous attraction on the island is a magnet for divers and boaters. The **Blue Lagoon** 30 is a shallow harbour area with a sandy bottom. The light reflected through the water gives it a brilliant azure colour (you can catch a fleeting glimpse of it from the ferry) that is reminiscent of the Caribbean. Boat trips are available from Valletta, Sliema, and many resorts on the northern coast of Malta.

There are plenty of places to swim or snorkel along the coast

WHAT TO DO

SHOPPING

Malta has been a trading island for millennia and merchants have always played an important role in its economy. Over the centuries, a number of traditional handicrafts have developed that now form the basis of the typical souvenirs you may want to take home with you.

WHERE TO SHOP

Malta is a great place for browsers. There are few major shopping malls and only a small number of shopping complexes (mostly located in Sliema, St Julian's and Valletta) where many major brands or chains, including Marks & Spencer and Benetton, have local branches. In contrast, the narrow streets of Valletta, Rabat and Victoria have a wealth of smaller shops.

Markets are also very popular and there is a regular timetable for every town. The major markets in Valletta are the clothing market on Merchants Street and the huge Sunday morning flea market at St James' Ditch. Most markets sell everything from fresh fruit and vegetables to collectibles, and even pets. Markets take place in the mornings; often the stallholders will have packed away by noon.

The Point

The Point Shopping Complex (www.thepointmalta.com; Mon–Sat 9.30am–7.30pm) is Malta's most modern and biggest shopping complex. It has an array of stores that include both high-street as well as designer brands, cafés, restaurants, and a kids' play area.

There are also two craft centres to explore. Here you can not only buy goods, but also see the craftspeople at work. Ta' Qali Village on Malta is situated near Mdina, and on Gozo you will find the craft centre at Ta' Dbiegi, outside the village of San Lawrenz, on the road to the Azure Window.

WHAT TO BUY

Lace. It was once commonplace to see the women of every village sitting out on their doorsteps making lace. Today, this remarkable handicraft is becoming rare – with few young women interested in learning the skill and cheap machine-produced lace flooding the market. On Gozo you will have a greater chance of finding women lace-making, but you will be able to buy items on Malta. The prices for fine hand-produced lace are reasonable and the quality is superb.

Sweaters and rugs. Knitted, woven and crocheted goods are abundant and offer good value for money. Women often sit out on summer evenings with knitting needles or crochet hooks working on items. Sweaters are popular and come in sizes to fit everyone from the smallest baby to the largest man. Woven rugs are another good practical buy. Made of wool or cotton, they are machine washable, easy to pack, and you will find numerous examples in Maltese family homes.

Silver and gold. Maltese artisans have been creating silver items for generations. You can find picture frames, spoons and christening mugs. The Maltese Cross is, of course, very popular, as a brooch or on a chain, and is an appropriate souvenir of your time here. Gold is also popular, as can be seen in the shops on St Lucia Street in Valletta.

Glass. You'll find handmade glass on both Malta and Gozo. The distinctive bright colours that swirl within each piece are introduced by adding powdered pigments when the glass is in

Maltese lace is renowned but only a few women, mostly in Gozo, still practise the art

its molten state. The range of items on offer includes vases, bowls and perfume bottles. The colours of the glass reflect the dominant hues of the islands: the blues and aquas of the sea, verdant greens of the spring landscape, and the beige of the sand and rocks in the summer sun. Mdina Glass can be found at the Ta' Qali Craft Centre, Malta. On Gozo, Gozo Glass has its studio at the Ta' Dbiegi Craft Village near Dwejra.

Pottery. Artefacts in the archaeological museums of each island bear witness to the longevity of pottery production here. Many items date from thousands of years BC, from Megalithic statuary to Roman amphora. Modern potters use both traditional and modern designs and you can buy pieces with a range of glazes.

Edibles. One theory about the origin of Malta's name is that it came from *melita*, the Greek word for honey. This indicates how important it was to the islands in ancient times. Today honey is used to sweeten a range of Maltese dishes and you can buy pots

Colourful glassware

of it to take home.

Cheese is one of the major products, particularly on Gozo, where it is still hand-produced on small farms. The small rounds of sheep's milk cheese called *gbejniet* ('j-bay-niet') are excellent and are served fresh, covered in herbs or pepper, or preserved in olive oil with sun-dried tomatoes.

Malta also produces oil and an unusual alcoholic liqueur. *Bajtra* is made from the juice of the prickly pear, which imparts a purple hue to the liquid, which is flavoured with herbs and honey.

ENTERTAINMENT

PUBS AND CLUBS

Malta has quite a sophisticated range of nightlife for such a small island. This centres on the resort areas of St Julian's, Paceville and Buġibba, where the large hotels and self-catering apartment blocks have been built. There are numerous bars and English-style pubs, such as **Fat Harry's** (Pjazza Walkway, St Paul's Bay, www.fatharryspub.com) and the **Dubliner** (Spinola Bay, St Julian's, www.irishpubmalta.com) along with an increasing number of wine bars like the luxurious **Tiffany Champagne and Cigar Bar** (Portomaso, St Julian's, tel: 9961 0163; www.tif

fanymalta.com). Many of these have live music or, at the very least, are equipped with superior sound systems.

Later in the evening you can head out to a club – there are many to choose from, including the Paceville stalwart **Havana** (St George's Road, Paceville, tel: 9964 8427), which has entertained generations of clubbers, to the more upmarket **Level 22** (Portomaso Tower, St Julian's, tel: 2138 6802; http://22.com.mt), which has stunning views across most of the island.

Most of the large hotels also have a schedule of entertainment, from dinner-dances to folklore programmes.

THEATRE AND MUSIC

Malta enjoys a healthy amount of theatre, ballet and concert recitals, particularly in the winter months. These are centred on venues in Valletta, such as the Manoel Theatre (www.teatrumanoel.com.mt) and the St James Cavalier Centre of Creativity (www.kreattivita.org), and take place at lunchtime as well as in the evening. The website of the Malta Tourist Authority, www.visitmalta.com, has a full list of activities taking place each month.

⊘ CASINOS

Malta has four casinos, offering a range of gambling opportunities. There's the newest Casino Malta in St. Julian's, which is open 24 hours a day; Dragonara Casino alongside the Westin Dragona hotel in St Julian's, set in a huge Greek Revival-style structure, built at the beginning of the 20th century as the summer residence of a local marquis; the Portomaso Casino adjacent to the Hilton Hotel; and the Oracle Casino at the New Dolmen Hotel in Qawra. To enter the casinos foreign nationals must be over 18 (take ID). The dress code is smart casual.

Manoel Theatre

OUTDOOR PURSUITS

There are only a few sandy beaches on the Maltese islands, whose coastlines are characterised by rocky stretches and narrow inlets. However, Malta is still popular with those who want to relax by spending time in the sun. Lido pools with sunbathing areas are cut into the rocks, providing seawater swimming pools in summer. Should you want to join the smart set, the Reef Club, St Julian's, near the Dragonara Casino, is considered the most fashionable and best-appointed lido. There is also The Lido near Tigne Point in Sliema, where many young locals and foreigners go to swim and mingle at all hours of the day and night.

The number of sandy beaches may be limited but there are endless numbers of places where you can swim or snorkel off the smooth rock coastline. A point to remember is that if you see a Maltese or Gozitan family picnicking and swimming along the shore, then that is a good place to swim.

BEST BEACHES

The largest beaches on Malta are **Mellieħa Bay**, **Għajn Tuffieħa**, **Golden Bay**, **Għadira** and **Ġnejna**, but just as much fun are the smaller places such as **Paradise Bay**, **Armier** and **Little Armier**. In Gozo try **Ramla** and **San Blas**. For swimming from the rocks, the best spots are around **Sliema**, **St Julian's**, **Paceville** and **St Thomas Bay**; and **Delimara** and **Peter's Pool** in the south. In Gozo the best swimming is around **Marsalforn** and **Xlendi** or in tiny coves like **Mġarr ix-Xini**.

SNORKELLING AND DIVING

With so many rocky inlets, it is not surprising that the Maltese islands are a snorkeller's heaven. The sea is clear and the fish plentiful, along with rock-dwelling creatures such as urchins and octopi.

The waters around the islands are some of the clearest in the Mediterranean with visibility between 40–50 metres (130–65ft). This, along with numerous natural features and wrecks to explore, make the islands popular destinations both with divers and snorkellers. Among the wartime wrecks are Royal Navy ships and aircraft.

Maltese law requires all divers to be over 14 years of age and have a medical certificate of fitness. Those

Topless tip

Although topless sunbathing is not permitted on the islands' public beaches, it may be acceptable on the private hotel beaches.

who have less than a PADI (Professional Association of Diving Instructors) advanced certificate or equivalent must dive with a certified instructor. Those who wish to dive independently will need a local dive permit. These are issued by the Malta Department of Health, through a local dive centre on Malta or Gozo.

If you wish to learn to dive, there is an excellent network of dive centres that offer training to professional levels. The centres are affiliated with the major certifying bodies, with PADI being the most common. The basic qualification, the Open Water certificate, takes five days to complete. On completion this will allow you to dive with an instructor to a depth of 18m (60ft), which opens up many dive sites.

For further information, contact the Federation of Underwater Activities (PO Box 29, Gzira GZR 10, Malta, tel: 9905 1306; www.cmas.org) or the Professional Association of Diving Instructors (61/2 Msida Seafront, Msida; www.padi.com).

OTHER ACTIVITIES

Most major hotels offer a full range of water sports, including jet skiing, windsurfing, sailing and 'banana rides'. The centres are generally open to non-guests. Many beach lidos have the same facilities.

If you want to take to the water under your own steam, you can hire anything from a kayak to a 10-berth 'gin-palace'. You will need a skipper's certificate for anything large – or you can hire a crew as part of the package and leave the hard work to them.

Active Pursuits. The islands offer facilities for a surprising number of sports and the climate is conducive to quite strenuous activities, especially in the spring and autumn months. Malta has an extensive regimen of competitive sporting events

Diving at the Santa Maria Caves, off Comino Island

throughout the year, including cycle races, marathons, biathlons and triathlons.

Climbing. With its rocky terrain and sheer cliffs, Malta is a climber's paradise. Sport climbing, bouldering, deep-water soloing and sea-level traversing can all be practiced on all islands. For more information, visit www.climbmalta.com.

Tennis. Most large hotels have tennis courts and these are often floodlit. Tennis is a very popular sport in Malta, with several community court complexes in towns and villages. The Marsa Sports Club (www.marsasportsclub.com) welcomes temporary members for golf, squash and tennis (tel: 2123 3851).

Walking. The southwest areas of the island and along the cliffs at Dingli take you to a rural Malta that you might otherwise not see. Many parts of Gozo have rural tracks where you can walk, and much of the coastline remains unspoilt. For details, see http://greatwalksmalta.com.

Ramla Beach, Gozo

CRUISES AND TOURS

Day Cruises. Take a tour of the Grand Harbour or a day cruise around the island with time for swimming and snorkelling. You can choose a state-of-the-art catamaran, a miniature cruise ship, a Turkish *gulet*, or a gaff-rigged schooner. An organisation called Captain Morgan offers the most comprehensive service, with several sizes of craft. They can even provide an underwater safari boat with Perspex keel, which allows you to enjoy the underwater environment without any risk of getting wet. Contact them at Dolphin Court, Tigne Seafront, Sliema, tel: 2346 3333, www.captainmorgan.com.mt.

Land Cruises. Take a four-wheel-drive safari to remote places. You'll see vestiges of the Malta of the past and find out just how diverse these islands are. Captain Morgan Cruises (see page 92) offers jeep safaris with an experienced leader. Drivers must be over 25. Gozo Jeep Tours (45 St Lucy Street, St Lucia,

Kercem, Gozo, tel: 9945 6809, www.gozo.com/jeeptours) offers tailor-made tours of the island, either for specific interests or general sightseeing.

CHILDREN

There are many attractions for children, who are made very welcome on the islands. Maltese children are treated with indulgence and will often be out late, especially in summer, wandering along the seafront with parents and grandparents who will stop for a drink at a café or bar.

The summer sun is strong, so always make sure that children have plenty of sunscreen protection at all times, even when they are playing in the water, and cover their heads with a hat.

Boat trips are always fun, whether it be across the Grand Harbour, out to the Blue Lagoon or around Gozo. There is a wealth of sea life to look out for as you go. A short trip into the Blue Grotto (Malta) or to the Inland Sea (Gozo) will fascinate children as they travel deep into the caves.

Take a *karrozin* ride around Valletta or Mdina. Children will enjoy being the centre of attention and being high above the crowds for a better view. Agree the price before setting off on the ride.

The colourful and lively *festas* are perfect for children. There is lots of music, and no one seems to mind how much noise they make. Spectacular firework displays are a highlight, but it's advisable to prepare the little ones for the noise.

Mediterraneo Marine Park (www.mediterraneopark.com), at Baħar iċ-Ċagħaq, offers up-close interaction with sea lions and dolphins, with feeding and educational programmes (see page 66). Popeye Village (https://popeyemalta.com), near Mellieħa (see page 69), is a great place to explore, and has an amusement park.

CALENDAR OF EVENTS

In summer hardly a weekend passes without a *festa* (see page 12) in one of Malta's towns or villages, when the local patron saint is celebrated with processions, band marches and fireworks. Other events include:

Carnival Traditionally held between the Friday and Tuesday preceding Lent, as a final exuberant festival before the religious fasting days begin. Noisy parades and fancy dress in Valletta, Malta, and in Nadur, Gozo.

Easter On Good Friday evening there are solemn religious processions in many villages marking the last hours of Christ's life. The biggest are in Mosta and Zejtun. On Easter Sunday church bells ring out joyfully.

End of April Malta International Fireworks Festival is celebrated annually at Valletta's Grand Harbour.

7 June Sette Giugno, a public holiday commemorating the bread riots of 1919 when starving Maltese took to the streets. A number of them were shot by British soldiers. **June** World Music Festival, an open-air festival with Maltese and Mediterranean music and dance held at Argotti Gardens, Floriana.

29 June The feast of St Peter and St Paul, known locally as Mnarija, takes place in Buskett Gardens, Rabat. It is a sort of harvest festival, with local produce on show and families gathering for picnics in anticipation of the folk singing that takes place after dusk.

Late July The Malta Jazz Festival in the Grand Harbour, with international jazz musicians.

15 August Santa Marija (to local people) but officially the Feast of the Assumption, is used by many young Maltese as an excuse for a holiday on Gozo.

8 September Victory Day (also the feast of Our Lady of Victories) marks the ending of the Great Siege of 1565. There is a presidential wreath-laying ceremony in Great Siege Square, Valletta.

October Notte Bianca (White Night): a cultural feast on Valletta's streets featuring performances, concerts, visual art exhibitions and all sorts of cultural activities. All state palaces and museums stay open until very late.

Sporting events include the Rolex Middle Sea Race, Malta Marathon, Garmin Malta Triathlon and Gozo Ultratrail.

EATING OUT

MALTESE SPECIALITIES

Maltese cuisine is essentially Mediterranean, though there are some outside influences. The many protectors who have come and gone have also played their part, leaving behind their own ingredients and culinary techniques.

The climate is an important influence on Maltese cuisine. The spring season has ample rainfall, which helps to ripen the vegetables, including cabbages, cauliflowers, potatoes and onions (potatoes and onions being important exports). There is very little rainfall in summer, but a sophisticated irrigation system allows a different range of crops to flourish (tomatoes, aubergines, melons and grapes), and salad crops are harvested throughout most of the year. Thus the Maltese cook has always worked with the seasonal gluts of various fruits and vegetables – even with the advent of freezers for storage, they still prefer to use whatever is fresh and in season.

Octopus salad

Maltese dishes traditionally take time to prepare. This is for a number of reasons, but largely because the lack of wood

Snail stew, known as bebbux

for stoves and fires in the past meant that creating a fire with a high heat was a false economy. In fact, many villages used a communal oven – usually the village bakery – to make more economical use of fuel. Because of this slow cooking method, many Maltese dishes do not transfer well to a restaurant menu, and this is in part why relatively few restaurants concentrate solely on local food. As the number of tourists began to grow, the Maltese opened restaurants serving what the visitors ate at home, hence the number of international menus to be found here. This is beginning to change and you can now find Maltese dishes on many restaurant menus.

The basics of Maltese cooking are excellent. Crusty bread is baked fresh every day – every town has a number of small bakeries so people can buy bread that is still warm. Often the bread is then drizzled with olive oil and rubbed with a tomato and sprinkled with salt, pepper and a few olives and capers. This simple dish, called ħobż biż-żejt (literally, bread with oil), provides a staple lunch for many farmers and fishermen during their working days, and is often served in restaurants as an appetiser. Also as an appetiser, aljotta (fish soup) is delicious, with its delicate lemony taste.

Cheese has long been produced from sheep's milk in Malta. It is mixed with salt and rennet and then dried (in the past this would have been done on the roof, under a net). Called *ġbejniet*, the cheeses can be young and soft or, as they mature, quite firm. On menus they are referred to as 'cheeselets'. *Ġbejniet* are often preserved with herbs and pepper, or sealed in a layer of olive oil.

The sea provides ample produce in the form of fish, crustaceans, octopus and squid. At the restaurants, you'll see what has been freshly caught as it will be sitting on ice. Some seafood is sold by weight before cooking. Smaller mixed fish are served for a set price, and are steamed or fried.

Over the centuries Maltese cooks learned to make use of bountiful fruits and vegetables, so as to make a little meat or other protein go a long way. They preserved meat as sausages flavoured with herbs and garlic, and mixed fish, meat or cheese with a variety of vegetables encased in pastry. *Lampuki* pie, one of the most popular Maltese dishes, is filleted dorado fish mixed with vegetables and wrapped in pastry. *Pastizzi a*re hot filo pastry snacks filled with ricotta cheese or a soft dried pea mixture. These are served at

⊙ RABBIT ON THE MENU

The land has historically provided a limited supply of protein. *Fenek*, or rabbit, is perhaps Malta's national meat and it is prepared in a number of ways. Most often you will find it on restaurant menus slow-cooked in wine and garlic. Another popular method is fried in oil. The favoured cooking method is rabbit stew, with sauce from the pot served with spaghetti for a first course and the rabbit to follow as a main course, served with plenty of wine.

Snails

When the autumn rains arrive, the islands see an abundance of snails. Many restaurants offer them as an appetiser, cooked in olive oil and garlic – mop up any surplus olive oil with your bread.

hole-in-the-wall cafés – great spots for lingering with local people.

Pasta is also widely used. Having travelled here from Sicily, pasta is considered as Maltese as it is Italian and traditional housewives make it fresh several times a week. A favourite is *ravjul* (ravioli) stuffed with cheese or mincemeat.

When they are not putting ingredients into pastry or pasta cases, Maltese cooks are stuffing them into other items. The islanders love *braġjoli* or beef olives – thin beef fillets stuffed with mincemeat, an onion and herb mixture, and smothered in an aromatic tomato-based sauce. Octopus (*qarnit*) and squid (*calamari*) are stuffed, as are the abundant peppers, aubergines and marrows. Rice, mincemeat, onions and tomato sauce are widely used when preparing stuffed vegetable dishes. Equally popular is *ross fil-forn* – oven-baked rice with mincemeat and tomato sauce. *Timpana* is an interesting combination of all three influences: a pastry pie filled with macaroni and a mixture of mincemeat, onions and tomato sauce.

SWEETS AND DESSERTS

Traditional sweets and desserts have a distinctly Eastern or Moorish influence and are often served as finger foods rather than in plate-sized portions, because they are so sweet. Try *imqaret*, deep-fried date-filled pastries, or *biskuttini tal-lewz* (macaroons). *Ħelwa tat-Tork* (Turks' sweets) is Malta's version of halva. *Kannoli*, deep-fried pastry stuffed with ricotta cheese, chocolate and candied fruit, originated in Sicily.

INTERNATIONAL CUISINE

Malta's restaurants serve a wide range of cuisines and the quality is of a high standard. Many restaurants take full advantage of the fresh produce of the islands. You are unlikely to be disappointed by the quality of vegetables that accompany many entrée dishes, although the variety may seem limited after a while. Steaks can be found in many restaurants served with various sauces. Veal (*vitello*) is also popular. French haute cuisine is available at a few of the more expensive restaurants.

You can eat in hundreds of trattoria-style restaurants offering pasta and pizza in a friendly informal atmosphere. Restaurateurs are increasingly using Maltese ingredients to give a different slant to pizzas – adding Gozitan cheese, for example, or Maltese sausage – and also to pasta, such as serving it with rabbit instead of the usual Bolognese or carbonara sauces.

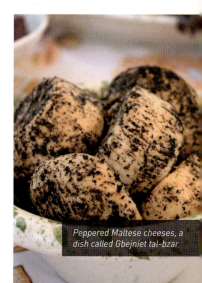

Peppered Maltese cheeses, a dish called Gbejniet tal-bzar

A few English pubs still serve pies and fish and chips, although the Maltese and Italian influence has overtaken this colonial vestige. There is also an increasing number of Indian, Chinese and other Southeast Asian restaurants, along with the occasional Greek restaurant or sushi bar.

DRINKS

Coffee is served in a range of Italian styles, especially espresso and cappuccino, and iced coffee is very popular in the summer. Fruit juices are excellent and refreshing, especially on hot summer days, and most are freshly made on the premises. The Maltese produce their own soft drink called Kinnie – a sparkling bitter, citrus drink – and a full range of international soft drinks is also available.

Some international beers are brewed locally under licence. The longest established brewery, however, brews Maltese beers. Cisk (pronounced *Chisk*) is the lighter; Hopleaf is equally refreshing but has a slightly heavier, nuttier taste.

Malta produces a range of wines, which have improved greatly over the past 20 years or so. The islands have introduced their own quality and origin certification system, the DOK (Denominazzjoni ta' Origini Kontrollata), similar to the AOCs of France. The wineries have invested heavily in modern machinery and techniques, taking

Maltese liquor

advice from French and Californian growers. The leading, most expensive wines are produced under the Meridiana label. Marsovin and Delicata are the producers of most wines found in restaurants and supermarkets. Italian and French wines are imported in great variety to supplement the domestic brands.

For after-dinner drinks, two rather unusual liqueurs are produced. Bajtra – said to be the favourite of the Knights – is made by distilling the juice of the prickly pear, which gives the finished drink a purple hue. The second, Tamakari, is a clear, sweet-flavoured liqueur.

HELP WITH THE MENU

To help you to order a meal in a restaurant, the list below contains a selection of the words (in Maltese) that you are likely to come across on a menu.

awwista lobster
bajd eggs
bigilla bean dip
braġoli beef olives
brunġiel aubergine, eggplant
dolce dessert
fagioli beans
faqqiegħ mushrooms
fenek rabbit
ġbejna Maltese sheep's milk cheese
għaġin pasta
ġobon cheese
ħaruf lamb
ħobż bread

ħut fish
laham taċ-ċanga beef
lampuka dolphin fish, special to Malta
larinġa orange
papra duck
patata potatoes
perżut ham
pixxispad swordfish
piżelli peas
qaqoċċ artichoke
tewm garlic
tonn tuna
uova eggs
vongole clams

PLACES TO EAT

We have used the following symbols to give an idea of the price for a three-course meal for one, including wine:

€€€ More than €50
€€ €35–50
€ Less than €35

MALTA

Valletta

Ambrosia €€€ *137 Archbishop's Street, tel: 2122 5923;* www.vallettarestaurant.com. Located in a street alongside the palace, this is an excellent restaurant with a menu that changes daily. Good starters and delicious main courses, all characterised by a seasonal Mediterranean slant. A fine wine list complements the food. Booking essential. Closed Sundays.

Blue Room €€€ *59 Republic Street, tel: 2123 8014.* Chinese restaurant close to the palace with charming staff and a reputation for serving the best of Cantonese dishes. Popular, so booking is recommended. Closed Mon. Wheelchair access.

Giannini €€€ *St Michael's Bastion (off Windmill Street), tel: 2123 7121;* www.gianninimalta.com. Located in a patrician house overlooking Marsamxett Harbour, with Manoel Island and Sliema across the bay. Ground-floor bar, and lift to the top-floor restaurant with panoramic views. There is a small terrace with six tables. Mediterranean fusion cuisine is the speciality of chef patron Aaron Degiorgio. Booking essential for dinner Fri and Sat. Wheelchair access.

Malata €€€ *St George's Square, tel: 2762 2733;* www.malatarestaurant.com. With an entrance on the square facing the palace, this restaurant has an excellent menu that appeals to politicians (parliament is across the road) and businessmen. Live jazz on Wed. Open daily lunch and dinner.

Palazzo Preca Restaurant €€€ *Strait Street 54, tel: 2122 6777*; http://palazzo precavalletta.com. Located in a 16th-century palazzo, this restaurant is run by two sisters, Ramona and Roberta Preca, and specialises in fish and pasta dishes. Romantic candle-lit dinners every Wednesday. Open Mon–Sat lunch and dinner. Sunday lunch only offered in winter; Sun dinner only in summer.

Da Pippo €€ *136 Melita Street, tel: 2124 8029*. Lunch only, but worth a visit for the generous portions of good, wholesome food cooked according to the chef's preference for Maltese dishes. Very popular, so booking is essential.

Rubino €€ *53 Old Bakery Street, tel: 2122 4656*; www.rubinomalta.com. Rated among the best in Malta. Opened in 1906, it is one of the oldest restaurants in Valletta offering good atmosphere, good food, good crowd. Menu changes daily but guaranteed to include Maltese and Mediterranean dishes. Mon lunch only, Tue–Fri lunch and dinner, Sat dinner only. Closed Sun. Booking essential.

Sliema

Barracuda €€€ *195 Main Street, tel: 2133 1817*; www.barracudarestaurant.com. Overlooking Balluta Bay and the sea, this is a pretty restaurant that is sometimes considered pricey, but nevertheless recommended by regulars. Fresh fish is a speciality. Booking advisable. Wheelchair access. Open daily for dinner.

La Cucina Del Sole €€ *Tigne Point, tel: 2060 3434*; www.lacucinadelsole. com.mt. Located in one of Malta's most modern and sophisticated estate projects, close to The Point shopping complex. The menu is varied, specialising in fresh fish and pizza. Don't miss their *calzone* (folded pizza). June–Sept Mon–Fri dinner, Oct–May Tue–Fri dinner. Open for lunch and dinner every Sat and Sun. Wheelchair access.

Piccolo Padre €€ *195 Main Street, tel: 2134 4875*; www.piccolopadre.com. A delightful pizzeria beneath Barracuda restaurant (see page 103). Great pizza and pasta in an informal setting, and popular with families. Maltese and Gozitan ingredients add extra interest to some dishes. A number of tables overlook the bay. Bookings taken except on Saturday nights. Expect to queue at weekends. Takeaway available. Mon–Sat dinner, Sun lunch and dinner.

La Rive € *33/34 Tigne Sea Front, tel: 2131 8323;* http://larivecafe.com. A popular café and winebar, with both outside and inside areas. Menu is varied and much-loved by regulars. Live gigs every Friday night during winter. Booking advisable at weekends; also open during the day. Wheelchair access. Live gigs every Fri. Open daily 8am–1am.

Vecchia Napoli €€ *255 Tower Road, tel: 2134 3434;* http://vecchianapoli. com. Definitely one of the most popular pizzerias on the islands, this casual eatery is consistently jam-packed with locals who love its hearty, flavoursome food. A good choice of pasta and salads is also available. Perfect for families. Booking is essential. Wheelchair access outside. Daily lunch and dinner.

St Julian's and Paceville

Hugo's Lounge €€ *St George's Road, Paceville, tel: 2138 2264;* www.hugos loungemalta.com. A delightful cross between a stylish cocktail bar and a respected restaurant, Hugo's promises great food in an upbeat atmosphere. The range of dishes on offer includes sushi, tempura and various Indian and Thai specialities. Very busy at weekends. Open daily.

Meat & Co €€€ *8 St George's Road, tel: 2138 5000.* Overlooking Spinola Bay, this restaurant is Malta's first self-proclaimed 'meat boutique'. The menu has various meat dishes, as well as gourmet salads and pasta dishes. Open daily. Book for the best tables.

Peppino's €€ *30 St George's Road, tel: 2137 3200.* This popular spot is favoured by locals looking for an inexpensive lunch accompanied by light wines. The restaurant serves Italian dishes and fresh fish, and also has a roof terrace. Crowded at weekends. Open daily 10am–11pm.

Sale e Pepe €€ *Portomaso Marina, tel: 2137 2918;* www.marinarestau rants.com.mt. Located in the popular and picturesque Portomaso Marina, this is an ideal choice for pasta and Mediterranean-themed meals.

Be sure to sample their delicious selection of *antipasti*. Open daily except Monday mornings.

San Giuliano €€€ *Spinola Road, tel: 2135 2000;* www.sangiulianorestaurant. com. Good-looking Italian restaurant with a view over St Julian's waterfront and often considered the smartest place on the island. Visiting film stars shooting on location in Malta often frequent it. The menu features many fish and seafood dishes. Booking recommended.

Tana del Lupo €€€ *58 Triq il-Wilga, Paceville, tel: 2135 3294.* Bustling and often hectic Sicilian restaurant. Excellent pasta dishes, but specialities are fish and seafood. Pavement tables outside in summer months. Booking advisable.

U Bistrot € *Balluta Bay, tel: 2311 2361;* www.ubistrot.com. A spot for great, wholesome food made with the freshest local ingredients. The menu includes pasta, salads and sandwiches. Get a table on the pavement and overlook the bay, or sit inside in elegant surroundings. Open daily. Wheelchair access.

Waterbiscuit €€€ *St George's Bay, tel: 2376 2225;* www.waterbiscuit. com.mt. Exceptional service and great food make this St Julian's restaurant stand out. Open 24/7 offering breakfast, lunch and dinner daily. Booking recommended at weekends. Wheelchair access.

Marsaskala

La Favorita €€ *Gardiel Street, tel: 2163 4113.* On the narrow road heading to St Thomas's Bay, this is an informal, family restaurant with a reputation for its consistently high standard of fish, served in an unpretentious way. Crowded and noisy at weekends, when booking is imperative. Open daily. Wheelchair access.

Grabiel €€€ *Mifsud Bonnici Square 1, tel: 2163 4194;* www.grabielmalta. com. Highly rated, high-priced family-run fish restaurant that has built up a serious local following of people who come here for the catch of the day, the octopus stew and, when in season, the *pasta rizzi* (spaghetti with sea urchins). The fish is sold by weight for some of the dishes. Crowded and noisy. Booking essential. Open lunch and dinner daily. Wheelchair access and facilities. Nice terraza.

Marsaxlokk

Ir-Rizzu €€ *52 Xatt Is-Sajjieda, tel: 9989 9965;* www.ir-rizzu.com. Friendly, family-run waterfront restaurant offering a range of dishes alongside its fresh fish specialities, which are extremely popular with regular customers. Booking is essential. Open daily for lunch. Wheelchair access.

Tartatun €€€ *Xatt Is-Sajjieda, tel: 2165 8089;* www.tartarun.com. Located on the Marsaxlokk seafront, this restaurant offers a great choice of fresh fish and crustaceans, including lobsters from a tank. A pricey but great place to eat. Lunch and dinner Tue– Sat, lunch only on Sun, closed Mon.

Mdina

Bacchus €€€ *1 Inguanez Street, tel: 2145 4981;* www.bacchus.com.mt. Set in the bastion walls of the city, with the entrance down a narrow side street. Large and popular, specialising in Maltese, French and Italian cooking. A good place for parties. Open daily 9am–midnight.

Medina €€€ *7 Holy Cross Street, tel: 2145 4004;* www.medinarestaurant malta.com. A pretty courtyard restaurant serving international food with British overtones. Dinner only. Closed Sunday. Wheelchair access.

De Mondion €€€ *Xara Palace Hotel, tel: 2145 0560;* www.xarapalace.com. mt. This is the rooftop restaurant of the gracious hotel perched on the bastion walls. Fine views of the countryside. The international menu and wines and the prices reflect the hotel's sense of status and occasion. Dinner only. No children under 12.

Trattoria AD 1530 €€ *Xara Palace Hotel, tel: 2145 0560;* www.xarapalace. com.mt. Simple trattoria with tables in the piazza outside the five-star hotel. A popular meeting place that serves pasta, pizza and simple Italian dishes. Open for lunch and dinner.

Rabat

L'Agape €€ *St Kataldu Street, tel: 2099 2209;* www.lagapemalta.com. A tiny restaurant located in the heart of Rabat, with an ever-changing menu that never fails to impress. Booking essential. Open for dinner Mon–Sat only. Closed Sun.

Café Wignacourt & Wine Garden €€ *Misrah San-Pawl, tel: 2749 4906.* A courtyard restaurant adjoining the Wignacourt Museum, it serves wholesome food and is particularly known for its *ftira* pizza. Events on every Thursday during the summer.

Il-Veduta €€ *Saqqija Square, tel: 2145 4666;* www.veduta.com.mt. Simple pizza and pasta restaurant hidden behind Mdina Gate car park. Wonderful view from its open terrace in summer. Has a casual atmosphere and is often crowded. Open daily. Wheelchair access. Free Wi-fi.

Mosta

The Lord Nelson €€ *28 Triq Il-Kbira 0, Mosta, tel: 2143 2590;* www.the lordnelsonrestaurant.com. Once a village corner bar, the Lord Nelson is now an attractive restaurant renowned for consistently good cooking and a menu unlike any other on the islands. This fashionable restaurant is popular with both the locals and tourists. Booking essential. Wheelchair access downstairs.

Qawra

Churchill's €€ *Triq il-Fliegu, tel: 2157 2480.* A typical Maltese restaurant that serves great fish dishes. Relaxed atmosphere and a great place to mingle with locals.

Tal-Kaptan € *Qawra Coast Road, tel: 2354 3842;* www.tal-kaptan.com. A fantastic pizza place the whole family will love. Great choice of dishes, including salads and grills, at reasonable prices. Big portions. Open daily for lunch and dinner.

St Paul's Bay

Gillieru €€€ *Church Street, tel: 2157 3480;* www.gillierurestaurant.com. Jutting out into the bay – with an open terrace that gets crowded in summer – this long-established fish restaurant is friendly and casual. Regulars praise the grilled fish, but there are also meat dishes, with traditional Maltese fare such as rabbit stew. Open daily for lunch and dinner. Wheelchair access.

Tarragon €€€ *21 Church Street, tel: 2157 3759;* www.tarragonmalta.com. One of the finest gourmet restaurants on the island, run by multi-award winning chef, Marvin Gauci. A great place to try something new. Booking essential at weekends. Open Mon-Sat dinner only, Sun for lunch only.

Mellieħa

The Arches €€€ *113 Main Street, tel: 2152 3460;* www.archesrestaurant. com.mt. In central Mellieħa, a large and brightly lit, colourful place with bustling service and large portions. Wide international menu. Booking advisable. Wheelchair access.

Giuseppi's €€ *25 St Helen's Street, tel: 2157 4882.* Spread over two floors, Giuseppi's is considered a fine example of a truly Maltese restaurant, both for decor and cooking. High standards maintained by an imaginative chef. Menu changes daily and is seasonal. Very popular, so booking is advised.

GOZO

Mġarr

Il-Kċina tal-Barrakka €€ *28 Triq Manuel de Vilhena, tel: 2155 6543.* Known to all as Sammy's, after the proprietor, this is where the crowd comes to dine casually on fresh pasta and fish. Many customers come over from Malta, as it is within walking distance of the ferry. Small, with an imaginative menu. Closed Nov–May. Open Tue–Sun for dinner. Booking essential. Wheelchair access.

Tmun Mgarr €€ *Martinu Garces Street, tel: 2156 6276;* www.tmunmgarr.com. Family run and quite casual, this is one of your best bets for fish dishes. Proprietors Leli and Jane will take you under their wing, offer a host of daily specials and numerous family favourites. Gets busy so it is best to book ahead. Closed Tue.

Victoria

Café Jubilee € *6, Library Street, tel: 2155 8921;* www.cafejubilee.com. Informal café dressed up to represent a 1920s French bistro. Wide range of snacks. Popular bar at weekends so it gets very crowded. Also has tables on the square. Open daily from 8am–midnight.

Il-Panzier €€€ *Triq il-Karita, tel: 2155 9979.* Gozo's most elegant – and most expensive – restaurant is hidden discreetly in a winding medieval street off It-Tokk. The limited menu is offset by the superior Italian cuisine. Courtyard dining. Lunch and dinner daily.

Patrick's Tmun €€€ *Europe Street, tel: 2156 6667;* www.patrickstmun.com. Attractive, busy restaurant where a young crowd gathers. The extensive menu includes a selection of dishes that are cooked in the Maltese manner. Seasonal fresh fish and seafood. Mon–Sat dinner only. Book at weekends. Closed Sun apart from winter months (lunch).

Ta' Rikardu € *4 Triq il-Fosos, in the Citadel, tel: 2155 5953.* A wine barrel topped with fresh bread and tomatoes signals the door into one of the oldest houses in the Citadel. Traditional Gozitan snacks make for light, cold lunches. The wine is made on the premises. This is an excellent, easy stop when exploring the walled city. Souvenirs, including honey and other Gozitan produce, are also available here.

Għarb

Jeffrey's €€ *Triq il-Għarb, tel: 9949 6230;* www.jeffreysrestaurantgozo.com. Excellent little trattoria, serving only seasonal dishes. Short menu featuring best local dishes including rabbit in wine and garlic or fresh fish of the day. Booking highly recommended as the place is small.

Salvina €€ *21 Frenc tal-Gharb, tel: 2155 2505*; www.salvina.eu. Pretty little restaurant set in a village house on a quaint, narrow street. There is a small courtyard for alfresco dining. Serves local and international cuisine. Open daily for lunch and dinner.

Marsalforn

Il-Kartell €€ *Marina Street, tel: 2155 6918*; www.kartellrestaurant.com. Housed in three inter-connected old boathouses, this popular restaurant has tables outside at the harbour's edge, weather permitting of course. Friendly atmosphere, good fish and local dishes, including pasta and pizza. Wheelchair access.

Ta' Frenc €€€ *Triq Għajn Damma, off Marsalforn Road, tel: 2155 3888*; www.tafrencrestaurant.com. Wide range of traditional Maltese and international cuisine, elegantly presented in a stylishly converted 14th-century farmhouse. Rustic interior with vaulted ceilings, and beautiful garden for alfresco dining. Regarded as one of the island's best restaurants, with prices to match. Open Wed–Mon for lunch and dinner. Wheelchair access and facilities.

Xlendi

The Boathouse €€€ *Xlendi Bay, tel: 2156 9153*; www.theboathousegozo.com. Located on the water's edge of the pretty bay of Xlendi, this restaurant has become one of the most talked about on the island thanks to its great menu and service. Open daily for lunch and dinner in high season.

Ic-Cima €€ *St Simon Street, tel: 2155 8407*; www.cimarestaurant.com. An amazing fish restaurant with an even better view. This family run establishment serves huge portions. Booking essential.

Xagħra

D Venue €€ *Victory Square, tel: 7955 7230*; www.dvenuerestaurant.com. A favourite amongst young locals, it offers great twists on traditional recipes. Halal, gluten-free and vegetarian options available. Regular entertainment from local and foreign bands. Closed Mon. Wheelchair access.

Oleander €€€ *10 Victory Square, tel: 2155 7230*. With some tables outside in the main square, the Oleander is known for its excellent local dishes, fish and steaks. Inside can be noisy as it is popular. Booking advisable. Wheelchair access.

Ta' Karolina €€ *Marina Street, tel: 2155 9675*; http://karolinarestaurant.com. Loved by locals and visitors alike, this popular restaurant is situated right on the seafront. The fresh food, reasonably priced wine and delightful ambience all contribute to a wonderful experience. Good value platters for two. Open daily for lunch and dinner. Wheelchair access.

Nadur

Maxokk € *St James Street, tel: 2155 0014*; www.maxokkbakery.com. Although it is a hole in the wall with no seating area, many consider Maxokk's Gozitan pizzas the epitome of the island's traditional cuisine. Order your pizza 30 minutes before pick up.

A–Z TRAVEL TIPS

A SUMMARY OF PRACTICAL INFORMATION

A

ACCOMMODATION (see also Camping and Youth Hostels, and for Recommended Hotels see page 134)

There is a full range of accommodation in Malta, from five-star hotels to a wide choice of self-catering options. All establishments offering accommodation are classified by the Maltese Hotel and Catering Establishments Board (HCEB) against a pre-determined set of criteria conforming to international standards. Standards of service are also rated, from De Luxe (the highest standard), to Gold, then Bronze (the lowest). www.visitmalta.com is a useful booking guide.

Hotels. Hotels are classified from one to five stars. Hotels in class one or two may not have rooms with private facilities. Always make enquiries before making a firm booking. Hotels in the higher star ratings will be well-equipped, though the rating does not reflect the quality of the facilities. Prices are normally quoted per person per night. When room rates are quoted, they include continental breakfast. High season, when prices are highest, is from mid-July to the end of September. Low season is from November to the end of March, but prices will rise at Christmas and Easter. Most hotels are available on holiday packages from Europe.

Many hotels offer full-board for relatively little extra cost. However, eating out is inexpensive on the islands and offers more of an experience.

Self-catering options. Self-catering is a popular choice, whether simple studios, apartments in small blocks, apart-hotels (with hotel-style accommodation and some units with kitchens), self-catering holiday complexes with restaurants, pools, etc., or renovated farmhouses in the countryside – a particular favourite on Gozo. Many of these are several hundred years old but renovated to provide spacious rooms, bathrooms and a pool. Most are set in picturesque locations. For farmhouse rentals on Gozo try Gozo Farmhouses (3 Triq i-Imġarr, Għajnsielem, Gozo, tel: 2156 1280, www.gozofarmhouses.com).

AIRPORT

Malta International Airport (MLT, www.maltairport.com) at Gudja, 10km (6 miles) southeast of Valletta, serves the whole of the archipelago. For flight enquiries tel: 5230 2000.

Taxis are available outside the arrivals terminal; buy a voucher at a desk inside the terminal and present it to the driver. It takes around 10 minute to get to Valletta (€15), 20 minutes to Sliema (€20) and 40 minutes to the Gozo Ferry Terminal (€40). Direct bus routes are available from the airport terminal to most main tourist destinations. For details, see www.maltairport.com.

B

BICYCLE RENTAL

Cycling is an easy and fun way to get around, particularly on Gozo with its quieter roads.

BUDGETING FOR YOUR TRIP

Malta and Gozo are inexpensive by European standards with food, excursions and attractions offering good value for money.

Car rental: (small vehicle) around €200 per week in August.

Entrance fee for state museums: €5–10.

Commercial attractions: around €7–12 for adults.

A three-course dinner for two without drinks in a moderate restaurant: €50.

Room rate during peak season in a moderate hotel, including breakfast, per person per night: €50–115. Full board can be as little as €12 extra.

Alcoholic drinks: €2.50; non-alcoholic drinks: €1.50

Horse and buggy tour: €15 for the first 30 minutes.

Island tour by bus: €20 per person.

Harbour boat tour: around €15 per person.

Open water dive course (five days): €340 for one accompanied diver; €16 for full equipment rental for the day.

There are several websites offering daily deals in Malta, which is ideal for getting money-off vouchers and discounts for meals, tours and even retail. Visit www.deal.com.mt or www.dealtoday.com.mt.

C

CAMPING

There is only one organised campsite on the Maltese islands, located at L'Aħrax in Mellieħa, one of the remotest and quietest parts of the country. Occupying approximately 12 acres of land, the campsite (www.maltacampsite.com) has numerous facilities, including showers and toilets. There are also dorms (for 6–10 people) that can be rented for around €15 per adult per night (based on 1-2 nights, €10 for longer stays).

CAR HIRE

Car hire is on par with most other European countries. In August, hiring a small car will cost around €200 per week if rented on arrival at the airport. When booking in advance online, the cost can be around €80. Collision damage waiver is fairly expensive (around €14 per day) but will be worth it for the peace of mind. Road conditions can make driving challenging (see page 117), although you will have greater freedom.

All the major car-hire companies have offices on the island. Some have desks at the airport, and it is possible to pick up a car on arrival. A number of the larger companies offer more competitive rates if you reserve from home.

Avis, tel: 2567 7550, www.avis.com.mt

Europcar, tel: 2576 1000, www.europcar.com.mtHertz, tel: 2131 4636, www.hertz.com.mt

Percius Car Hire, tel: 2144 2530, www.percius.com

Meli Car Rentals, tel: 2258 0300, www.meligroup.com

Most companies have age limits between 25 and 70. Your national driving licence will be acceptable. If you rent in Malta you can take the car to Gozo on the ferry.

CLIMATE

Malta has a typical Mediterranean climate with hot, dry summers and mild winters. Even winter days may have long bouts of sunshine. The short spring is characterised by sunny days with cool breezes. By May the rain ceases until October and the temperature rises. Summer heat can be exacerbated by warm winds from North Africa, but the situation is mitigated by sea breezes, which cool off the coastal areas.

Sea temp	J	F	M	A	M	J	J	A	S	O	N	D
°F	58	58	58	62	65	70	75	76	77	72	67	62
°C	14	14	14	16	18	21	24	26	25	22	19	16

Air temp	J	F	M	A	M	J	J	A	S	O	N	D
Average daily max.												
°F	59	60	62	66	71	82	83	84	82	77	69	63
°C	15	15	16	19	23	27	30	31	28	24	20	17
Average daily min.												
°F	49	49	51	54	59	65	70	71	69	63	57	53
°C	9	9	10	12	15	19	21	22	20	17	14	11

CLOTHING

You will obviously need swimwear for the beach or pool, but walking around town in swimwear is unacceptable. In spring or autumn, bring a couple of extra layers – warmer trousers and a sweater or jacket for chillier days (it can be breezy) and to wear in the evenings when it can get cooler. In the winter you need a layer of warm clothing and protection against rain. In the evening, casual clothes are acceptable in most establishments. However, if you intend to eat at some of the finer restaurants, the code words are 'smart casual' – a jacket for men (ties are rarely required) and 'dressy' ensemble for women is appropriate. Enquire about dress code when you book.

If you intend to visit churches make sure that you are appropriately dressed. This means no swimwear, and both sexes must have their shoulders covered. Men should take off hats when entering a church.

CRIME AND SAFETY

Malta is relatively crime-free, but petty crime such as handbag snatching is on the increase in tourist areas and it pays to take precautions. Put your valuables in the hotel safe if there is one. Don't carry large amounts of cash, and never leave valuables unattended on beaches or visible in a car. Walk only on well-lit streets at night. If you are a victim of crime, report it to the police immediately.

D

DRIVING

Driving is not for the faint-hearted, but can be rewarding since you can make your own timetable and visit major sites when large tour groups have departed. Points to remember are the general poor driving ability of the nation, and the sheer number of vehicles. Lane discipline is poor; drivers pull out of junctions in front of you or turn off without using indicators; running red lights is common. Vehicles are often in poor condition, resulting in feeble acceleration, noise and belching exhaust fumes. Road signs for major attractions are intermittent, and many streets look identical, which can make map-reading a challenge. However, Malta is such a small island that you are never really lost. Most local people are approachable and happy to point you in the right direction.

If you are bringing in your own car be sure to remember your driving licence, insurance certificates including Green Card and registration documents. Customs make thorough checks of car documents on entering and leaving Malta.

Road Conditions. Drive on the left and overtake on the right. Roads have not yet been given official classifications but on most maps are either red (major), yellow (secondary), or white (country). Road conditions vary widely. Major roads can be good but prone to subsidence in coastal areas. Minor or country roads may be poor, with numerous potholes. Roads in white on maps will be dirt tracks. Drive cautiously and be prepared for the unexpected.

Rules and Regulations. There are speed limits of 80kph (50mph) on highways and 50kph (30mph) in urban areas, although many people drive much faster. Always be prepared to travel much slower on country lanes. Be constantly vigilant. Drivers and all passengers must use seat belts. Motorcycle riders must wear a crash helmet.

In most towns and villages there are one-way systems, making a direct route through town impossible.

If you are involved in an accident, call the police (tel: 112) and traffic wardens (tel: 2132 0202). Do not move your vehicle until they arrive. This causes mayhem for other road users but it is important to obtain a police report to settle any claims that may arise.

Fuel Costs. Petrol costs around €1.40 per litre for unleaded. Fuel stations are open Mon–Sat 7am–6pm. Service stations have automatic pumps that take €5 or €10 notes for petrol service after hours.

Parking. It may be hard to find a space in main tourist resorts and the capital. Street parking is permitted unless there are posted restrictions – these include residents-only parking. A yellow line at the roadside means No Parking. Most new larger hotels have car parks for guests' use but smaller, older hotels may not. Leaving a car on the street is not a problem as far as security is concerned (don't leave valuables in your car), but finding a space near your hotel could be.

Parking in Valletta is difficult and controlled by the council through a colour-coded system – it is advisable to pay strict attention to it. Green boxes are purely for residents, while blue boxes can be used by visitors between 7am–7pm. White boxes are usable at all hours. There is an underground car park near the bus station, and parking along the city wall by Marsamxett Harbour. It is best to leave a car at one of these places and enter the city on foot. Most major sites outside Valletta have a parking area, often manned by unofficial parking attendants wearing peaked hats, who orchestrate your arrival and departure for a small sum – €1 is usual. Traffic control and enforcement of parking restrictions are the duties of local wardens, who wear brown uniforms with a yellow reflective sash.

Road Signs. Malta uses international road signs, and many will be instantly understandable. Official signs are in English.

If You Need Help. In the event of a breakdown, there are many mechanics on Malta who will tow your vehicle and make on-the-spot repairs for a reasonable price, but it is advisable to speak to your car rental agency about who you should contact.

E

ELECTRICITY

The electrical supply is 240 volts/50 cycles and the British style 3-pin, 13-amp socket is standard.

EMBASSIES AND CONSULATES

Australia: Australian High Commission, Ta'Xbiex Terrace, Ta'Xbiex, tel: 2133 8201, www.malta.embassy.gov.au

New Zealand: Consulate, Villa Hampstead, Oliver Agius Street 16, Attard, tel: 2143 5025, www.nzcmalta.com

United Kingdom: British High Commission, Whitehall Mansions, Ta'Xbiex, tel: 2323 0000, email: bhcvalletta@fco.gov.uk

US: Embassy of the United States, Ta' Qali National Park, Attard, ATD 4000, tel: 2561 4000, www.malta.usembassy.gov

EMERGENCIES

In an emergency, dial 112 for all services and tel: 2132 0202 to report traffic accidents.

G

GAY AND LESBIAN TRAVELLERS

Malta is a conservative Catholic country, and same-sex relationships could be shocking for many residents. However, there is a noticeable gay community, and a small number of gay-friendly bars can be found in the tourist resort areas of Paceville, St Julian's and Valletta. The Gay Malta website, www.gaymalta.org, carries all of the latest information.

GETTING THERE

By Air. The national carrier is Air Malta (www.airmalta.com). It operates a number of services to Europe and North Africa, and has regular flight connections with the following cities: London Heathrow/Gatwick, Birmingham, Bristol, Cardiff, Exeter and Manchester in the UK; Amsterdam, Brussels, Paris, Geneva, Frankfurt, Rome and Vienna among others. All these connections allow for easy onward travel from destinations in the US (Air Malta has partnership agreements with TWA via London Gatwick or Milan Malpensa), Canada, South Africa, Australia and New Zealand. The flying time from London is around three hours.

Other airlines that operate scheduled services to Malta include: Air France, Alitalia, Austrian Airlines, British Airways, KLM and Lufthansa. Low-cost airlines include Ryanair, Easyjet, Jet2 and Thomas Cook.

Gozo has no airport, but a seaplane provides a scheduled service from Valletta's Grand Harbour to Mġarr harbour, Gozo.

Charter flights. Several operators, including Thompson, fly to Malta from Europe all year round, with extra flights in summer but can be booked only with hotels/self-catering accommodation as part of the package. As subsidiaries of Air Malta, Belleair Holidays (www.belleair.co.uk) and Malta Direct (www.maltadirect.com) offer year-round flights and package holidays to the Maltese islands.

By Sea. Malta is linked by ferry services with mainland Italy and Sicily. The much quicker connection is from Pozzallo (90 minutes) and Catania (2.5 hours) in southern Sicily with a high-speed car/passenger service that sails daily, weather permitting. The service extends to Reggio Calabria, Italy, weekly. It is operated by Virtu Ferries, Malta (tel: 2206 9022, www.virtuferries.com). The car ferry has good facilities, cabins and a restaurant.

A number of cruise lines offer Malta on their Mediterranean itineraries. These include Fred Olsen Lines, Holland America Line, Royal Caribbean and Cunard.

By Car. If you travel with your own vehicle no bond is required as long as you are staying for less than three months. A Green Card is necessary to extend your insurance cover so your vehicle is covered for third party while you are driving overseas. Be prepared for customs to check your documents and insurance cover as you enter the islands.

By Rail. Rail services connect to the ports of ferries (see page 121) sailing to Malta from Italy and Sicily (Catania). It is a time-consuming way to travel, although Italian trains always run on schedule.

GUIDES AND TOURS

A number of reliable companies offer daily tours around the island or to Gozo. These normally include a guide, but the quality of guides varies. The Malta Tourism Authority licences a number of guides; contact them for more details. Captain Morgan Cruises offer a full programme of tours by air, sea or on land (Dolphin Court, Tigné Seafront, Sliema, tel: 2346 3333, www.captainmorgan.com.mt). Gozo Jeep Tours (45 St Lucy Street, St Lucia, Kercem, Gozo, tel: 9945 6809, www.gozo.com/jeeptours) offer tailor-made tours of the island, catering for specific interests or just general sightseeing.

H

HEALTH AND MEDICAL CARE

Health concerns. There are no serious health concerns to worry about when you visit Malta. In summer the sun is strong, and even early or late in the season it is sensible to take precautions against sunburn. Limit your time in the sun during your first few days, apply sunscreen regularly, and carry clothing to cover your skin should it begin to burn. Wear a hat and sunglasses. Don't forget that the effects of the sun can penetrate water – so you still need protection in the pool or the sea. Always make sure that young children are adequately protected while playing. Mosquitoes can be a problem; always carry insect repellent with you.

The standard of general medical facilities is good and all medical personnel speak excellent English. There is one general hospital on Malta and one on Gozo. There are also several health centres open 24 hours a day for minor health problems/accidents. In an emergency dial 196 for medical assistance.

Mater Dei Hospital, B'Kara By-pass, B'Kara MSD 2090, tel: 2545 0000.

Gozo General Hospital, Ghajn Qatet Street, Victoria, tel: 2156 1600.

Vaccinations. No vaccinations are normally needed unless you are arriving from a cholera- or yellow fever-infected area and are within six days of leaving that area.

Water. Although it is safe to drink the tap water, it does not always taste pleasant. Bottled mineral water is available everywhere.

Insurance. Nationals of EU countries are entitled to reciprocal health care in public hospitals and from medical practitioners who are part of the national health care service. You need a European Heath Card (EHIC), obtainable online at www.ehic.org.uk, and also from post offices in the UK. However, this does not cover all eventualities and you should also have a comprehensive insurance policy that covers accidents and illness, among other things. Malta also has a reciprocal health care agreement with Australia.

A range of over-the-counter drugs is available to treat everyday ailments, and pharmacists will be able to advise you about minor ailments. Most prescription drugs are available on the islands. A letter from your doctor will be needed for a prescription to be issued by a Maltese doctor. Pharmacists are open during normal store hours and a few also open on Sunday mornings (for more details, visit http://health.gov.mt).

L

LANGUAGE

There are two official languages in Malta: Maltese or *Malti* – the national language, an ancient language that is related to Arabic and written in the Roman script – and English, which is spoken fluently by most of the population.

Many street names and signs in major towns are printed in both Malti and English, but not all, so it helps to have a basic understanding of how certain letters and words are pronounced. This will certainly help you when you need to ask someone for directions, although local people will usually go out of their way to make sure that you are heading in the right direction.

ċ – like *ch* in *child*
g – as in *good*
ġ – like *j* in *job*
għ – silent
h – silent, unless at the end of a word (*h* as in *hello*)
ħ – *h* as in *have*
j – like *y* in *year*; **aj** like *igh* in *high*; **ej** like *ay* in *say*
q – almost silent – like a very faint *kh*-sound; a bit like the Cockney glottal stop in 'ain't *it*'

x – like *sh* in shop

z – *ts*

ż – *z*

Common Town and Site Names

The Maltese like to hear at least the names of their towns and villages pronounced properly. Here is a list of the main sites mentioned in this book.

Birżebbuġa bir-zeb-boo-ja

Borġ in-Nadur borj in nah-dure

Buġibba boo-jib-ba

Ġgantija j´gan-tee-ya

Għadira add-eer-ra

Għajn Tuffieħa ayn tuff-ee-ha

Għar Dalam ar da-lam

Għar Lapsi ar lap-see

Għarb arb

Ħaġar Qim ha-jar-keem

Marsamxett mar-sam-shet

Marsaxlokk mar-sash-lok

Mdina im-dee-na

Mellieħa mel-lee-ha

Mġarr im-jar

Mnajdra im-niy-dra

Naxxar nash-shar

Qala ah-la

Qawra ow-ra

Qormi or-mee

Siġġiewi sij-jeer-wee

Tarxien tar-sheen

Xagħra sha-ra

Xewkija show-kiya
Xlendi shlen-dee
Żebbuġ zeb-booj
Żejtun zay-toon

A Few Everyday Expressions

Maltese *pronunciation*
good morning **bongu** *bon-joo*
good evening **bonswa** *bon-swa*
yes **iva** *ee-va*
no **le** *le*
please **jekk jogħġbok** *yek yoj-bok*
thank you **grazzi** *grat-see*
excuse me **skużi** *skoo-zee*
Where is...? **Fejn hu...?** *fayn oo*
right **lemin** *le meen*
left **xellug** *shel-loog*
straight ahead **dritt il-quddiem** *drit il ood-deem*
How much? **Kemm?** *kemm*

Numbers

0 **Xejn** *shayn*
1 **Wieħed** *wee-hed*
2 **Tnejn** *tnayn*
3 **Tlieta** *tl-ear-ta*
4 **Erbgħa** *er-ba*
5 **Ħamsa** *hum-sa*
6 **Sitta** *sit-ta*
7 **Sebgħa** *seb-ba*
8 **Tmienja** *tmeen-ya*
9 **Disgħa** *dis-sa*
10 **Għaxra** *arsh ra*

M

MAPS

The Malta Tourism Authority prints a number of maps and short guides that are perfect for exploring the major towns on foot. If you require a map for touring by car, there is a range available from tourist shops. None of these maps has comprehensive coverage of the one-way systems in each town or village, but they are helpful for getting from place to place.

MEDIA

Newspapers. The main Maltese English-language newspapers are *The Times* (www.timesofmalta.com) and *The Independent* (www.independent.com.mt). Both tend to concentrate on local issues, covering international news in brief. Most major hotels and newsagents sell the major British dailies on the evenings of the day they are printed. The *International Herald Tribune* is also available, but major American newspapers are more difficult to find.

TV. Most hotels offer a satellite service with CNN and the BBC, German, Italian, French and Arabic channels.

MONEY

Cash. The official currency of Malta and Gozo was the Maltese Lira but on 1 January 2008 changed to the Euro, bringing Malta in line with other European Union countries. Notes are denominated in 5, 10, 20, 50 and 100; coins in 1 and 2 euros and 1, 2, 5, 10, 20 and 50 cents.

There is no limit to the amount of foreign currency that can be imported into Malta, provided large sums (over €10,000) are declared on arrival. Customs officials have the right to search and question departing passengers with regard to how much currency they are carrying.

Currency Exchange. Currency can be exchanged at banks, government accredited currency bureaux, hotels and some shops. Banks offer the best exchange rates.

ATMs and credit cards. A large number of banks have ATMs that accept international debit or credit cards – look for the familiar symbols. Some machines impose an extra charge on withdrawals from foreign banks. Credit cards are widely accepted in hotels, shops and restaurants. You will even be able to buy goods from some market stalls with them. An increasing number of businesses also accept payment by international debit card (Maestro); you will see signs in the window advertising the facility.

O

OPENING TIMES

Opening hours on the islands can be complicated. Winter hours are longer than those in summer, when the heat becomes oppressive in the afternoon. Longer working days usually begin on 1 October and end on 16 June. If you have any important business to attend to, it would be best to do it in the morning when banks, offices, shops and government buildings are definitely open.

All commercial activity stops at lunchtime at all times of year, so the Maltese can observe the tradition of a substantial midday meal followed by an afternoon siesta.

Banks. Generally Mon–Fri 8.30am–2pm, Sat 8.30–noon.

Bars, cafés and restaurants. Bars open in the evening and, in tourist areas, close around 1am. Cafés open for coffee and snacks around 8am and close between 6pm and 1am. Restaurants open for lunch, generally noon–3pm, and dinner 7–11pm.

Government offices. Open 16 June–30 Sept Mon–Fri 8am–noon-1.30pm; 1 Oct–15 June 8am–3pm.

Museums. Museums are generally open Mon–Sat 8.15am–5pm, Sun 8.30am–1pm.

Shops. Mon–Fri 9am–1pm and 4.30–7pm, Sat 9am–1pm. Many shops in tourist areas do not close for lunch and are open longer hours, especially in summer. The law forbids most Sunday trading except for newsagents, although this law is currently being relaxed with places like Bay Street Shopping Complex (www.baystreet.com.mt) in St Julian's opening 10am–10pm at weekends as well.

P

POLICE

The police are friendly and approachable, and will certainly offer assistance if you are lost. They wear blue uniforms in summer, and black (with peaked caps) in winter. Police vehicles are blue and white. Some officers travel by scooter.

There are police stations in each major town but not all are staffed 24 hours a day. In an emergency dial 112.

Report traffic accidents to the police and do not move your vehicle until they arrive (see also Driving). To report traffic accidents, tel: 191 or 2132 0202.

Police headquarters are at St Calcidonius Square, Floriana, Malta, tel: 2122 4001 or 2122 4007 Gozo, tel: 2156 2040.

POST OFFICES

Malta has a relatively efficient postal system; usual opening hours are Mon–Sat 7.30am–1pm. The post offices at 305 Qormi Road, Qormi, and at the airport are open Mon–Sat until 8pm.

In Gozo the main office is at Triq ir-Repubblika 3, Victoria; opening hours are Mon–Fri 8.15am–4.30pm, Sat 8.15am–12.30pm.

Post boxes are positioned along the sides of the streets and are painted red. They may either be inserted into the wall or round freestanding structures.

PUBLIC HOLIDAYS

On the public holidays listed below, tourist shops and restaurants will be open, but local shops, some supermarkets, offices and banks will all be closed.

Public holidays in Malta and Gozo are:
1 January New Year's Day
10 February St Paul's Shipwreck Day
19 March St Joseph's Day
31 March Freedom Day
March/April Good Friday, Easter Sunday and Easter Monday
1 May Labour Day
7 June Commemoration of 7 June 1919 (Sette Giugno)
29 June St Peter and St Paul Day (L'Imanarja)
15 August Feast of the Assumption
8 September Victory Day
21 September Independence Day
8 December Feast of the Immaculate Conception
13 December Republic Day
25 December Christmas Day

R

RELIGION

The Maltese population is predominantly Roman Catholic but there are Anglican, Baptist, Buddhist, Jehovah's Witness, Jewish, Methodist, Mormon, Muslim and Orthodox places of worship on Malta.

T

TELEPHONES

The international country code for Malta and Gozo is 356 followed by the number. When making an international call always dial 00 before the country code.

Go is the provider of most landline services. Most hotels offer direct-dial facilities, but they are priced at a premium and can be extremely expensive.

Roaming charges are very much in-line with the rest of Europe, and holiday SIM cards are available for short stays. There are three main mobile suppliers in Malta: GO, Vodafone and Melita.

TIME ZONES

Malta operates on Central European Time (CET), one hour ahead of Greenwich Mean Time in winter and two hours ahead from the end of March to the end of October. In summer the following times apply:

New York	London	**Valletta**	Jo'burg	Sydney	Auckland
6am	11am	**noon**	1pm	10pm	midnight

TIPPING

Tipping for good service is expected. Some restaurants include a service charge on the bill but most do not, in which case a tip of 10–12 percent is usual. For other services:

Taxi driver: no tip

Porters: 40 cents per piece of luggage

Chauffeur: €2

Hairdresser: €2.

TOILETS

Public toilets are to be found in most major towns – look for them in market squares, harbours or near bus stations. Standards of cleanliness vary. Malta's museums and historical sites are all striving to provide facilities even if they are in the form of portable toilets. You can use the facilities in bars. If there is an attendant, a small tip is appropriate.

TOURIST INFORMATION

The **Malta Tourism Authority (MTA)** is responsible for tourist information and has a number of excellent leaflets and brochures to help visitors make the most of their trip.

The MTA head office also acts as an information centre: Auberge d'Italie, Merchants Street, Valletta CMR 02, Malta, tel: 2291 5440/2, www.mta.com.mt. Local tourist information bureaux are:

Malta: Malta International Airport arrivals lounge, tel: 2369 6073/4; Valletta Waterfront, Pinto Wharf, tel: 2122 0633.

Gozo: Independence Square, Victoria, tel: 2291 5452/3.

The mta also has offices in the following countries:

UK: Malta Tourist Office, Unit C Parkhouse, 14 Northfields, London SW18 1DD, tel: (020) 8877 6993, www.visitmalta.com.

US and Canada: c/o Malta Mission to the UN, 249 East 35th Street, New York NY 10016, tel: 212-2130944, www.visitmalta.com.

TRANSPORT

Buses. The local bus service on Malta is comprehensive, reliable and relatively cheap – a single ticket costs €1.50 (winter), €2 (summer) and €3 (night service). The company that runs Malta's public transport is **Malta Public Transport** (www.publictransport.com.mt; 2122 2000) More than 400 buses run daily, on over 80 routes, between 5.30am and 11pm (there is also a night service Fri–Sat and holidays).

The 7-day Explore Card (€21) offers unlimited travel on Malta and Gozo (day and night). The 12 Single Day Journeys Card offers flexibility with reduced fares for 12 journeys, is valid for a year and can be shared. Tickets can be bought as you board a bus, while travel cards should be purchased online and at selected outlets. Valletta's bus terminus is just outside the City Gate.

Gozo buses have a terminus at Main Gate Street in Victoria. The buses operate on a circular route. A service connects with the ferry timetable. There are about 15 different routes in Gozo to various localities on the island. For tickets and timetables, see www.publictransport.com.mt.

Taxis. White taxis have meters and should charge the government-controlled rates that should be on display in the cab. If a driver is reluctant to use his meter, agree a price before starting your journey.

Many local car hire companies, such as Percius (www.percius.com; tel: 2144 2530) and Wembleys (http://wembleys.com; tel: 2137 4141), have chauffeur-driven black Mercedes that are no more expensive than taxis and can be pre-booked. They are also available for all-day hire, for sightseeing.

Ferry. Marsamxett Steamferry Service (www.vallettaferryservices. com), Dolphin Court, Tigné Sea Front, tel: 2346 3862, runs a passenger-only service between Sliema and Valletta. The service operates daily, every 30 minutes, €1.50 one-way. Service may be reduced on Sundays and public holidays.

Horse-drawn buggies *(karrozin)*. These offer tours rather than journeys. Official fares are €7 for 30 minutes and €2 for each subsequent 30 minutes, but these are rarely enforced and a fare should be agreed before you start your journey. You will find them in Valletta, Mdina and Sliema.

Between the islands

Air. There is no direct air link between the islands. A small seaplane flies from the Grand Harbour to Mġarr, Gozo, but does not connect with airline schedules. There is no connection with the airport. It is used by commuters and visitors on excursions.

Sea. The Gozo Channel Company (tel: 2210 9000, www.gozochannel. com) operates passenger and light-vehicle ferries from Ċirkewwa (on the western tip of Malta) to Mġarr on Gozo. The passenger ferry sails at least once every hour, but timetables change with each season. Tickets are purchased on return from Mġarr in Gozo.

The Comino ferries (http://cominoferries.com) provide transport to Malta and Gozo. A number of private boats offer tours of Gozo or the Blue Lagoon on Comino from Ċirkewwa or resorts along the northern coast of Malta, many of them during the summer only.

V

VISA AND ENTRY REQUIREMENTS

Entry Requirements. The following do not need an entry visa for stays of less than three months: citizens of all European Union countries, Australia, New Zealand, Canada, the United States, Israel, Japan, Singapore and South Korea.

If you want to extend a trip beyond three months, a written request must be made to the Commissioner of Police, Police Headquarters, Floriana, before the end of the three-month period.

Customs. The same customs regulations apply in Malta as in the rest of the European Union. Check with a Malta Tourism office if you are in doubt about specific items.

W

WEBSITES AND INTERNET ACCESS

Websites are given in the contact details of individual attractions, hotels and restaurants throughout this guide. However, here are a few general websites that may help you to plan your trip.

www.visitmalta.com
www.malta.com
www.choosemalta.com
www.holiday-malta.com
www.visitgozo.com
http://heritagemalta.org
www.maltainsideout.com
www.mta.com.mt/

WEIGHTS AND MEASURES

Malta uses the metric system.

Y

YOUTH HOSTELS

You can find a list of the available youth hostels at www.visitmalta.com/en/hostels.

RECOMMENDED HOTELS

Malta has a large range of hotels, with a number of fine five-star establishments complementing hotels of other standards. Choices around the capital are limited since the resort areas have grown around the coastal bays – originally at St Paul's and Bugibba, more recently at St Julian's and Sliema.

Prices are reasonable by European standards. The smaller budget hotels may have more limited facilities, but all will be spotlessly clean. Most large hotels will offer prices for half-board or full-board that are good money-saving options, but with the range and value of eateries around the island, it would be a shame to limit yourself to the hotel restaurant for the whole of your stay.

Prices are generally quoted per person per night with breakfast included. All rooms in three-star establishments and above must have private bathroom facilities.

Prices rise during the summer months and holiday periods such as Christmas and Easter when it would be wise to make a reservation before you travel.

The symbols below give an indication of peak season prices per person per night, including breakfast.

€€€   **more than €165**
€€   **€100–165**
€   **Less than €100**

MALTA

Valletta

Castille € *348 St Paul Street, Valletta VLT 01, tel: 2124 3677;* www.hotel castillemalta.com. Close to Upper Barrakka Gardens, this hotel is set in a converted 17th-century town house. Some of the 38 rooms have balconies. Facilities include two restaurants, a coffee shop and a bar.

Grand Harbour € *47 Battery Street, Valletta VLT 01, tel: 2124 6003;* www. grandharbourhotel.com. Small, 30-room hotel with great harbour views. Rooms are small, clean, and have television. Facilities include a restaurant and sundeck.

Osborne €€ *50 South Street, Valletta VLT 01, tel: 2124 3656;* www.osborne hotel.com. This well-appointed budget hotel is located in the city centre. All 63 rooms have air-conditioning and television. Facilities include a pleasant bar, restaurant and small roof spa pool.

Phoenicia €€ *The Mall, Floriana VLT 16, tel: 2122 5241;* www.camp bellgrayhotels.com. This fine building is ideally placed, being only a few minutes' stroll from the centre of Valletta and from the main bus station, which has services to the rest of the island. Facilities include three restaurants, two bars, a hairdressers and an outdoor pool.

Sliema, St Julian's, Paceville

Corinthia Marina €€€ *St George's Bay, St Julian's STJ 02, tel: 2370 2000;* www.marinahotel.com.mt. An attractive hotel with all 189 rooms overlooking the bay. Friendly and well-appointed with a selection of restaurants and cafés. It also shares beach facilities with its elegant neighbour, the Corinthia San Gorġ (see below).

Corinthia San Gorġ €€€ *St George's Bay, St Julian's STJ 02, tel: 2137 4114–6;* www.corinthia.com. At the entrance to St George's Bay on the water's edge, this member of the Corinthia Group is ideally placed for enjoying the sea and the sun. Facilities include a wide choice of restaurants, excellent health spa, swimming pools and a popular beach lido.

Fortina Spa Resort €€ *Tigne Sea Front, Sliema SLM 15, tel: 2346 0000;* www. hotelfortina.com. Situated in Marsamxett harbour with excellent views of the Valletta skyline, this ever-expanding hotel is a few minutes' walk to Sliema's shopping streets, the waterfront, and The Point, Malta's largest shopping complex. An all-inclusive, 220-room hotel with attractive landscaped gardens, four restaurants, two pools and three spas that offer a variety of health treatments.

Golden Tulip Vivaldi €€ *Dragonara Road, St Julian's STJ 06 tel: 2137 8100;* www.goldentulipvivaldi.com. In the heart of Paceville, close to the sea and the Dragonara Casino, this large modern hotel has 263 rooms (many with sea views), conference facilities, a rooftop pool, a fitness centre and a selection of restaurants.

Hilton Malta €€€ *Portomaso, St Julian's STJ 02, tel: 2138 3383.* This imposing, 294-room hotel sits on the headland at St Julian's. The facilities include five restaurants, three bars, a shopping arcade, garden, gym, squash and tennis courts, indoor and outdoor pools and a disco. Wheelchair access throughout.

Hotel Juliani €€ *St Julian's STJ 06, tel: 2138 8000;* www.hoteljuliani.com. Deluxe, 44-room boutique hotel, overlooking a picturesque bay. Offers a delicious breakfast to wake up to. Has a rooftop pool, fashionable restaurants and free Wi-fi.

Intercontinental Malta €€€ *San Wistin Street, St Julian's STJ 02, tel: 2137 7600;* www.ihg.com. Located a short distance from the sea, this large modern hotel has six restaurants and cafés, two pools (one at rooftop level), conference facilities and a popular health club. And it's at the heart of the entertainment district. 451 rooms.

Le Méridien St Julians Hotel and Spa €€€ *39, Main Street, Balluta Bay, St Julian's STJ 1017, tel: 2311 0000;* www.lemeridienmalta.com. Positioned halfway between Sliema and St Julian's, Le Méridien merges the concepts of boutique and spa to create a sharp yet relaxing atmosphere. All 276 rooms and suites have a view. Includes four restaurants, a spa with indoor heated pool, conference facilities and a shopping arcade.

Preluna Hotel and Towers €€ *124 Tower Road, Sliema SLM 01, tel: 2133 4001;* www.preluna.com. This large, 280-room hotel on the main coastal road at the eastern end of Sliema is popular with tour groups. Many of the rooms have sea views. Facilities include three restaurants, three bars, indoor and outdoor swimming pools (the outdoor pool is across the street), gym, sauna and water sports, including a scuba diving school. Wheelchair ramps throughout.

Radisson Blu Resort €€ *St George's Bay, St Julian's STJ 02, tel: 2137 4894;* www.radissonblu.com. Situated on the edge of St Julian's and Paceville, within easy reach of the nightlife yet comfortably removed from it. Facilities include four restaurants, five bars, a gym, private beach, sauna, indoor and outdoor swimming pools, tennis courts and powered water sports. All 252 rooms have views of the sea.

The Waterfront €€ *The Seafront, Gzira SLM 03, tel: 2133 3434;* www.water fronthotelmalta.com. Nicely positioned facing Valletta on the waterfront from where daily cruise boats set out. All 116 rooms have a view. Has a rooftop swimming pool and two restaurants. Only a few minutes' walk into Sliema.

Westin Dragonara Resort €€€ *Dragonara Road, St Julian's STJ 02, tel: 2138 1000;* www.westinmalta.com. A stylish family hotel set in landscaped gardens on its own peninsula, close to Dragonara Casino and St Julian's entertainment district. Most rooms have sea views. There are good restaurants, swimming pools, conference facilities and a children's club. The 340 rooms include 25 suites and two penthouses.

Birżebbuġia

Water's Edge € *Summit Square, Birzebbugia BBG 2310, tel: 21650036;* www. watersedgemalta.com. Just 10 minutes away from Malta's International Airport, this modern and stylish hotel is located on the edge of an idyllic bay, hence the name. All 40 rooms have a view and free Wi-fi. Includes two restaurants.

Mdina and Central Malta

Corinthia Palace €€€ *De Paule Avenue, Attard BZN 05, tel: 2144 0301;* www. corinthia.com. A luxury, 155-room resort hotel in the centre of the island, the Corinthia Palace, with its superb landscaped gardens, is the dowager of Malta's hotels. Guests can use the beach and water sports facilities at the sister hotel, Corinthia San Gorġ in St Julian's (see page 135).

Xara Palace Relais and Chateaux €€€ *Misraħ il-Kunsill, Mdina MDN 02, tel: 2145 0560;* www.xarapalace.com.mt. A beautiful boutique hotel lo-

cated in the bastions of the medieval citadel, and a perfect place for a romantic get-away. The rooms are furnished to the highest standards. Facilities include two restaurants, a bar and a sundeck. 17 suites.

St Paul's Bay, Mellieħa Bay and Qawra

Dolmen Resort €€ *St Paul's Bay SPB 05, tel: 2355 2355;* www.dolmen. com.mt. A large and popular, easy-going family hotel facing the sea, located midway between quiet Qawra and Buġibba with its bustling night-life. The facilities include swimming pools, a tennis court, a gym, and the Oracle Casino, with a slot machine hall, as well as the traditional gaming room. 413 rooms and suits.

Gillieru Harbour € *Church Square, St Paul's Bay SPB 01, tel: 2157 2720;* www.gillieru.com. On the seafront next to a fishing harbour and the church square of St Paul's Bay, this is in an ideal location for strolling to the restaurants and bars. Fifty rooms are accompanied by two restaurants, a bar, pool, games room and water sports. 74 rooms.

Golden Sands Radisson Blu Resort €€€ *Golden Bay, Mellieha, tel: 2356 1000;* www.radissonblu.com/en/goldensandsresort-malta. This is one of the island's top hotels, with stunning views of the golden sands below, the glistening Mediterranean, and the unspoilt surrounding country-side. The hotel has 329 modern rooms, eight bars and restaurants, a spa, business centre, private beach and water sports.

Mellieha Bay € *Mellieha Bay, Għadira SPB 10, tel: 2357 0000;* www.mellieha bayhotel.com. This large hotel faces Għadira, the biggest sandy beach on Malta. Bus routes to Valetta or Ċirkewwa for the Gozo ferry pass di-rectly outside. The 313-room hotel is popular with tour groups. Facilities include a restaurant, four bars, swimming pools, tennis courts, water sports, a garden and nightclub. There is also a diving centre on site.

Paradise Bay € *Ċirkewwa SPB 10, tel: 2152 1166;* www.paradise-bay.com. A large, 217-room hotel on the western tip of Malta, overlooking the ferry dock for Gozo. There is a popular dive facility here, but no res-taurants or bars around the hotel. Facilities include two restaurants, two bars, a private beach, indoor and outdoor pools, tennis courts and a shopping arcade.

Seashells Resort at Suncrest €€ *Qawra Coast Road, Qawra, tel: 2157 7101;* www.seashellsresortmalta.com. This all-inclusive hotel provides a get-away-from-it-all location. Facilities include water sports and a children's pool, as well as a professional diving centre. It was thoroughly renovated in 2015.

Selmun Palace € *Salman, Mellieħa SPB 10, tel: 2152 1040;* www.gala hotels.com. Situated on a hill high above Mellieħa Bay to the west of Malta, this hotel is comprised of an 18th-century castle with an extensive but sympathetic modern addition. Facilities include a gourmet restaurant in the castle's former chapel, a bar, indoor and outdoor swimming pools, games room, gym, private beach and tennis courts. 154 rooms, six suites in the castle.

Sunny Coast Resort € *Qawra Bay SPB 1981, tel: 2157 2994;* www.sunny coast.com.mt. Large family-orientated holiday hotel facing the bay. Only a stroll away from the busy centre of Buġibba, it offers restaurants, pools and children's entertainment. Self-catering apartments are also available.

GOZO

Calypso € *Marsalforn, tel: 2156 2000;* www.hotelcalypsogozo.com. Long-established, 100-room hotel ideal for families. Located only steps from the sea and the promenade, it has restaurants, tennis and squash courts.

Cornucopia € *10 Ġnien Imrik Street, Xagħra VCT 110, tel: 2155 6486;* www. cornucopiahotel.com. Pretty hotel with 50 rooms and suites in the centre of the island, based in a converted farmhouse. Lots of atmosphere. Facilities include two swimming pools, a restaurant, bar, games room and hairdresser. There are also self-catering bungalows and converted farmhouses.

The Grand € *Triq Sant Antnin, Għajnsielem GSM 104, tel: 2156 3840;* www. grandhotelmalta.com. An attractive hotel on the hillside above the port of Mġarr with its fishing boats, ferries and fish restaurants. Most of the

46 rooms have balconies; many have sea views whilst others overlook the countryside. Family suites also available. Restaurant and small rooftop pool.

Kempinski San Lawrenz & Spa €€€ *Triq ir-Rokon, San Lawrenz, GRB 104, tel: 2211 0000;* www.kempinski.com/en/gozo/hotel-san-lawrenz/. Located outside the tiny village of San Lawrenz and near the Inland Sea, this comfortable hotel has excellent facilities plus a Thalgo spa with marine algae therapy and an Ayurveda centre. There are conference facilities, pools, restaurants and floodlit tennis courts. 106 rooms and suites.

San Andrea € *Xatt ix-Klendi, Xlendi VCT 115, tel: 2156 5555;* www.hotel sanandrea.com. Small 28-room hotel on the seafront with pleasant, attentive service. Some of the rooms have sea views. Simple restaurant.

St Patrick's € *Xatt ix-Xlendi, Xlendi VCT 115, tel: 2155 1866;* www.vjborg. com. Beautifully located on the harbour in the picturesque cove at Xlendi, this hotel takes its design features from traditional buildings. Some of the rooms have windows and balconies overlooking the inner courtyard, others have views over the bay. Facilities include a restaurant, bar, splash pool and whirlpool.

Ta' Ċenċ €€€ *Sannat VTC 112, tel: 2219 1000;* www.tacenc.com. In a secluded country location but with a private beach, Ta' Ċenċ offers delightful countryside accommodation. Facilities include a restaurant, bar, two swimming pools, excellent health spa, tennis courts and whirlpool. Be sure to explore the nearby dolmen and other ancient remains. 83 rooms and suites.

COMINO

Comino € *Island of Comino, SPB 10, tel: 2152 9821;* www.cominohotel. com. Comino island's only hotel, with 95 rooms, two restaurants, a pool, health club, tennis courts, games room and hairdresser. Closed end Oct–Easter.

INDEX

INSIGHT ⊙ GUIDES POCKET GUIDE

MALTA

First Edition 2017

Editor: Tom Fleming
Author: Lindsay Bennett
Head of Production: Rebeka Davies
Picture Editor: Tom Smyth
Cartography Update: Carte
Update Production: AM Services
Photography Credits: Bigstock 4MC, 51,
53, 56, 71, 74, 79; Dreamstime 35; Getty
Images 1, 4TC, 4ML, 5T, 5MC, 13, 15, 28,
41; iStock 6R, 23, 31, 43, 91; Malta Tourism
Association/Clive Vella 58; Public domain 19;
Shutterstock 6L, 67; Sovereign Order of St
John 21, 24; Sylvaine Poitau/Apa Publications
4TL, 5TC, 5M, 11, 33, 36, 39, 45, 47, 48, 61, 62,
65, 69, 72, 76, 81, 82, 95; Viewing Malta 5M,
5MC, 7, 7R, 16, 54, 85, 86, 88, 92, 96, 99, 100
Cover Picture: Shutterstock

Distribution
UK, Ireland and Europe: Apa Publications
(UK) Ltd; sales@insightguides.com
United States and Canada: Ingram
Publisher Services; ips@ingramcontent.com
Australia and New Zealand: Woodslane;
info@woodslane.com.au
Southeast Asia: Apa Publications (SN) Pte;
singaporeoffice@insightguides.com
Hong Kong, Taiwan and China:
Apa Publications (HK) Ltd;
hongkongoffice@insightguides.com
Worldwide: Apa Publications (UK) Ltd;
sales@insightguides.com

**Special Sales, Content Licensing
and CoPublishing**
Insight Guides can be purchased in bulk
quantities at discounted prices. We can
create special editions, personalised jackets
and corporate imprints tailored to your
needs. sales@insightguides.com;
www.insightguides.biz
All Rights Reserved
© 2017 Apa Digital (CH) AG and
Apa Publications (UK) Ltd

Printed in China by CTPS

No part of this book may be reproduced,
stored in a retrieval system or transmitted in
any form or means electronic, mechanical,
photocopying, recording or otherwise,
without prior written permission from Apa
Publications.

Contact us
Every effort has been made to provide
accurate information in this publication,
but changes are inevitable. The publisher
cannot be responsible for any resulting loss,
inconvenience or injury. We would appreciate
it if readers would call our attention to any
errors or outdated information. We also
welcome your suggestions; please contact
us at: hello@insightguides.com
www.insightguides.com